Candlesticks
Explained

Martin J. Pring on Technical Analysis Series

Candlesticks Explained

Martin J. Pring

McGraw-Hill
New York Chicago San Francisco
Lisbon London Madrid Mexico City Milan
New Delhi San Juan Seoul Singapore
Sydney Toronto

Library of Congress Cataloging-in-Publication Data

Pring, Martin J.
    Candlesticks explained / by Martin J. Pring
        p.   cm.
    ISBN 0-07-138401-4
    1. Stocks—Prices—Charts, diagrams, etc. 2. Commodity exchange—
charts, diagrams, etc. 3. Investment analysis. 4. Stock price forecasting.
4. Stocks—Prices—Japan—Charts, diagrams, etc. I. Title

    HG4638 .P75 2002
    332.63'2042—dc21   2002003900

McGraw-Hill

A Division of The McGraw·Hill Companies

    3 4 5 6 7 8 9 0   AGM/AGM   0 8 7 6 5 4

p/n 139857-0   part of ISBN: 0-07-138401-4

The sponsoring editor for this book was Stephen Isaacs and the production super-
visor was Clare Stanley. It was set in New Baskerville by MacAllister Publishing
Services, LLC.

Printed and bound by Quebecor/Martinsburg.

This publication is designed to provide accurate and authoritative information in
regard to the subject matter covered. It is sold with the understanding that neither
the author nor the publisher is engaged in rendering legal, accounting, or other
professional service. If legal advice or other expert assistance is required, the services of a competent professional person should be sought.

–From a Declaration of Principles jointly adopted
by a Committee of the American Bar
Association and a Committee of Publishers

McGraw-Hill books are available at special quantity discounts to use as premiums
and sales promotions, or for use in corporate training programs. For more information, please write to the Director of Special Sales, Professional Publishing,
McGraw-Hill, Two Penn Plaza, New York, NY 10121-2298. Or contact your local
bookstore.

 This book is printed on recycled, acid-free paper containing a minimum of
50% recycled de-inked fiber.

Contents

Preface

This book forms part of the series *Martin J. Pring on Technical Analysis*. Like all the others in the series, its main value lies in the CD-ROM enclosed in the back cover. This little disk contains a complete multi-media presentation of the subject matter contained in the workbook.

Years ago I published videos on technical analysis, but the CD_ROM format is far superior. Not only does each chapter play as a continuous presentation but also the need to fast forward or rewind is eliminated. Instead, the user can click on any subject matter in the contents and move instantly there. This format also allows for an interactive quiz, so the user can quickly move through multiple choice questions or chart examples, all of which are scored at the end. In this way, you can easily discover any area that needs brushing up. The only title in the series that does not contain a quiz is *How to Select Stocks Using Technical Analysis*.

The series itself is designed to expand on several of the subjects covered in the fourth edition of *Technical Analysis Explained*. Each of the book/CD-ROM combinations takes the reader into greater depth on the individual subjects. Diagrams and theoretical concepts are explained and then adapted to practical marketplace examples. It is normal in presentations of this nature to indicate the strong points of any indicator or concept, but these presentations also advise you of any known weaknesses of pitfalls they may have.

Technical analysis is the art of identifying trend reversals at a relatively early stage and riding on that trend until the weight of the evidence shows or proves that the trend has reversed. The objective of this series is to present a substantial amount of that evidence in the form of indicators and concepts, so that readers of the workbooks and viewers of the CD-ROMs will be in a stronger position to identify such trend reversals. Please take note of the fact that technical analysis deals in probabilities, *never* certainties. Armed with the information in this series, the probabilities should now move heavily in your favor.

With that in mind, good luck and good charting!

Martin J. Pring
Sarasota, Florida

**To my brother, Richard Pring,
and his wonderful partner, Heather**

Acknowledgments

This book would not have been made possible without the work of my friend Steve Nison, who introduced the concept of candlesticks to the West with his two ground breaking books *Introduction to Candlesticks* and *Beyond Candlesticks*. While many of the techniques described here are my own, a substantial amount of this material is based on the concepts he outlined in his two books.

The year 2002 will see the publication of eight of my books by McGraw-Hill. Six of these form part of the Martin J. Pring on Technical Analysis Series, a series of multi-media CD-ROM/workbook tutorials. None of this would have been possible without the help of several key people.

In particular I would like to thank Jimmie Sigsway, my wonderful mother-in-law, whose support of our busy family allowed both me and my wife, Lisa, to allocated sufficient time to work on this project.

Without a doubt, a might thanks goes to Jeff Howard of Interactive Software Design, who has, as usual, pulled out all the stops and done a superb job creating the installation program and multimedia programming for the CD-ROM tutorial contained at the back of this book.

I would also like to thank many of our subscribers, workshop attendees, and purchasers of our CD-ROMs, whose kind and constructive comments have greatly encouraged me to expand the "Pring library."

Above all, a special thanks goes to my wife, Lisa, who, despite multiple pressures from major domestic construction work, minding the kids (including me), cooking the meals, and maintaining our Web site at pring.com, was still able to deliver the artwork for this book on time.

Introduction

I first heard about candlesticks in the 1980s, when my publisher, McGraw-Hill, asked me to review a proposal for a book that they had received. My conclusion was that the concept would never sell in the United States and that it was not worth a book. How wrong I was! Today, no charting package is complete without the candlestick option, and it is a technique practiced by a huge proportion of traders.

The effect of candlesticks is very short term in nature, so the massive growth of intraday and swing traders has made this ancient Japanese art an obvious one to adopt. Originally used to plot daily rice prices in eighteenth-century Japan, candlesticks are now used to analyze virtually anything that moves in freely traded markets.

To plot them correctly, candlesticks require the high, low, open, and closing prices for a session, be it a 10-minute, 1-hour, daily, weekly, or monthly bar. They do not provide information that is any different from a Western-style bar chart plotted from the same data. However, they display this same information in a different, more graphic, way, which makes it possible to spot certain price patterns and characteristics that are associated with changes in trend.

My definition of technical analysis is that it is the art of identifying a trend reversal at a relatively early stage and riding on that trend until the *weight of the evidence* shows or proves that the trend has reversed. I believe that candle charting should be used in conjunction with Western charting techniques. The words *weight of the evidence* have been emphasized because candlesticks are one piece of evidence in the technical jigsaw, along with trendlines, oscillators, moving averages, and so on. That is why I believe candle analysis should not be used in isolation but rather in conjunction with Western charting techniques.

1

The book starts off with the basics of candlestick charting itself, in which the various patterns have been broken down into reversal and continuation types. A whole chapter has been devoted to the integration of candlesticks with Western charting techniques. Additional, though less well known, Japanese charting methods, such as Three-Line Break, Renko, and Kagi, have been included to round out the presentation. The interactive quiz contained on the CD has also been reproduced at the end of this book, so that readers can conveniently test themselves on the material covered if they so wish.

To anyone wishing to make instant profits in the financial markets, this book will prove to be a disappointment. However, to those willing to take the time to study, make mistakes, and gain experience, the practice of candlestick charting will substantially increase the odds of financial success.

Martin J. Pring

I

Basic Candle Principles

1

A Brief History of Candlestick Charts

Japanese candlestick charts are probably the oldest type of charting technique used for price prediction. Dating back to the 1700s, the earliest forms of candlestick charts were originally used to predict rice prices. In 1750, a wealthy Japanese merchant, Munehisa Homma, began trading at his local rice exchange in Sakata using his own personal candlestick analysis. Homma became a legendary rice trader and amassed a huge fortune. Folklore says he executed over one hundred successive winning trades! Today's Japanese candlestick methodology is credited to Homma's trading principles as he applied them to the rice markets.

Although the West only recently adopted candlestick charting as a legitimate tool, this technique has now become very popular, especially with swing and day traders. Since candlestick charting reflects short-term phenomena, its forecasting abilities are also short-term in nature, rarely lasting more than 10 days, often much less. There are numerous ways to interpret this fascinating technique, and we will take a look at several and will use candlesticks in conjunction with other accepted technical tools.

Candlestick shapes and formations were given descriptive names by the Japanese traders, partially due to the military environment of the Japanese feudal system during this era. Many of these names are battle- or military-oriented, such as *counterattack lines* and *three advancing white soldiers*. But many names are also derived from the descriptive language that the Japanese use to express everyday objects and occurrences. When you see patterns such as a *hammer, shooting star,* or *hanging man,* their visual interpretation is very close to the actual descriptive meaning. Here is a good example: The Western trading term *gap* is called *window* in candlestick jargon. You will become more familiar with this descriptive terminology as you work with these patterns. Also, while working through this tutorial or any other candlestick information, remember that candlestick charts do not provide price targets. Candlesticks should always be analyzed in relation to what occurred historically on the chart and also should always be confirmed by other proof of technical confirmation, such as a confirmation in a price pattern or a moving-average crossover.

Basics of Candle Construction

Whether you find candlestick charts to be more visually appealing than the standard bar chart, the information displayed in candlestick charts is identical to that displayed in bar charts (see Fig. 1-1). Each method contains four common elements for construction. These are the *open, high, low,* and *closing* price for a given time period. It is the *way* candlesticks are displayed (i.e., their shapes) that makes them unique and gives them special interpretive powers.

When I speak of *prices,* I am referring to a particular time period, such as a day, week, or month. While candlesticks can be plotted for any period, they are synonymous with daily data; therefore, this is the time frame I will concentrate on in this book. Since candle patterns on daily charts only have

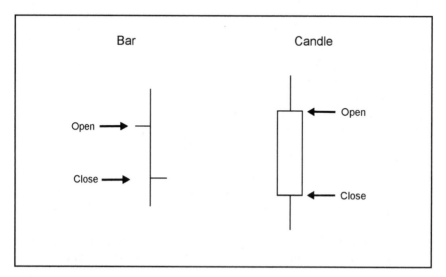

Figure 1-1   Candle versus bar chart.

short-term implications, they are best used for trading purposes, as opposed to investing, which requires a longer time horizon.

Bar charts treat the opening, closing, high, and low prices more or less equally, while the candlestick method places special emphasis on the opening and closing prices. However, how people *feel* about a security when they start the trading day, and their attitudes toward the security when the session closes, are of paramount importance to candlestick enthusiasts.

The rectangle portion of the line, called a *real body*, represents the range of the opening and closing price, such as we see in Fig. 1-2. The top of the rectangle represents the higher of the two prices, and the bottom the lower. For example, if the close was $10 and the opening was $9.50, the top part of the rectangle would be plotted at $10 and the lower part at $9.50.

You may be asking the question, "How can we tell which is the opening and which is the closing?" The answer lies in the color of the rectangle. If the rectangle is white, or empty, as in the example on the left, the lower part of the rectangle represents the opening price, and the top part represents the closing price (usually a bullish period). Alternately, if the rectangle is black, or filled-in, the opening price is at the top and the closing price at the bottom (usually a bearish period).

One thing that confused me when I first looked at candles was that I started to think that black candles meant down days and white candles meant up days. That, of course, is not true, since it is possible for a black

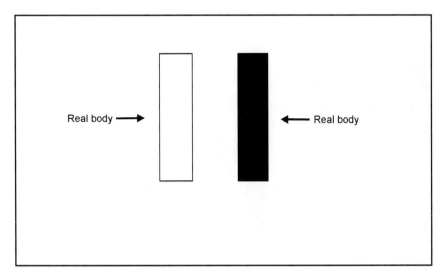

Figure 1-2   Real bodies.

candle to close above yesterday's close or even above yesterday's high. What makes a candle black is that the close for the period plotted at the bottom of the real body is always below the open, which is plotted at the top. For white candles, the open is at the bottom and the close at the top.

But what about the high and the low for the day? The thin lines that appear above and below the real body (Fig. 1-2a) represent the high and low and are known as *shadows*. The line above the real body is the *upper shadow* and the one below it the *lower shadow* (see Fig. 1-2b). A candle having no upper shadow (Fig. 1-3) is said to have a *shaven head*, whereas one with no lower shadow is a *shaven bottom*. Although the Japanese view the real body as the decisive price movement, shadows are mostly thought of as superfluous price fluctuations.

As I mentioned, both Western and Japanese types of charting use four types of information. The major difference between Western bar charts and candles is that candles *require* all four pieces of data, the opening and closing prices together with the high and low. Without all this information, it is impossible to plot a candle. Western bar charts only require the close, the high, and low: the opening price is optional.

Since the four pieces of data that go into the construction of a candle can fluctuate considerably, there are numerous variations as to how they are displayed on the chart. Some possibilities are shown in Fig. 1-3. If the opening and closing prices are identical, the real body will appear as a horizontal

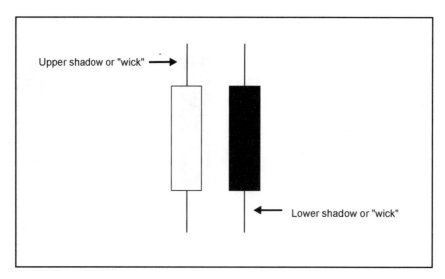

Figure 1-2a   Shadows (Wicks).

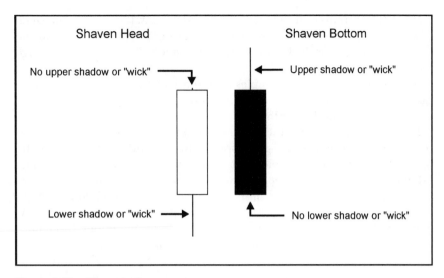

Figure 1-2b Shaven bodies.

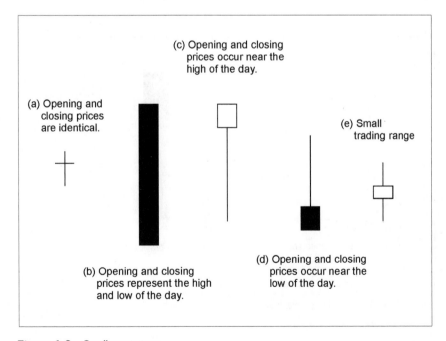

Figure 1-3 Candle variations.

line (a). If they represent the high and low of the day, there will be no shadows (b). It is possible for the opening and closing prices to occur near the high of the day (c) or the low of the day (d). Finally, the day's trading range may be very small (e).

Some of these extreme examples have special names and can have forecasting characteristics in their own right, just as bar charts have outside days, key reversal days, and so forth.

For instance, a candle in which the opening and closing prices are very close to the low and high, respectively, and the range between the open and close is large is called a *long white line*, shown on the left in Fig. 1-4. When the close is near the low and the open near the high, or the opposite, it is known as a *long black line*. To qualify as a long black line, though, the range between the opening and the closing must be relatively large. As mentioned earlier, long white lines tend to be bullish and long black lines bearish. Later, we will see that these individual patterns often form part of a price pattern, just as do bars in a bar chart. The principal difference is that candle patterns are usually very short term in nature and, therefore, take a much shorter time to complete. The qualification of a long line can only be determined with reference to the other candles that have appeared in the recent past. For example, what may be considered a long day in a

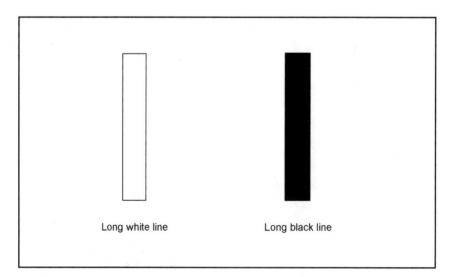

Long white line   Long black line

Figure 1-4   Long white and black lines.

very quiet and subdued market may be far less "long" than in a very volatile period, when a typical trading range for a day is much greater. Generally speaking, to qualify as a long day, a real body should be at least three times the size of the previous day's real body (Fig. 1-5). The long real body is not usually sufficient to justify a bullish or bearish stance on its own. What it does is to say, "if it is a white long real body, then here is a very strong statement by the bulls," or, "if the white real body is short, here is a very strong statement by the bears."

Consequently, when patterns are combined with other technical phenomena, they emphasize the strength of other characteristics. For example, if a trendline break develops on the day of a long real body, the penetration stands a far better chance of being valid, as shown in Fig. 1-6. In effect, the long day gives the trendbreak greater credibility. The same thing could be said for a long body that breaks a support or resistance area, completes a price pattern, or crosses a reliable moving average.

Long real bodies that develop after a prolonged uptrend or downtrend are often a first sign that the trend is in the process of reversing. Again, it is important to make sure the long real body is confirmed by subsequent price action.

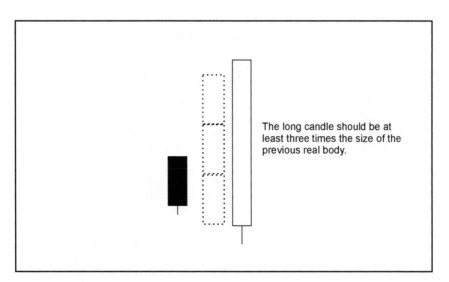

The long candle should be at least three times the size of the previous real body.

Figure 1-5   Long lines in proportion.

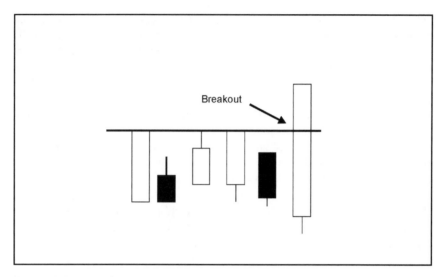

Figure 1-6 Long white line breakout.

Basic Candle Pattern Building Blocks

The candle patterns in Fig. 1-7a–d are among the most essential individual candlestick lines for building candle patterns. A *doji* is a trading session where the opening and closing prices are the same, or very close to it (Fig. 1-7b). Doji lines come in different types, and their interpretation depends on where the opening and closing prices appear in the context of the entire trading range. I feel that since the opening and closing prices are identical or extremely close, a doji represents a session of indecision. When dojis appear in trading ranges, they reflect an environment in which buyers and sellers are temporarily in balance and are, therefore, of little significance. However, when they appear after an advance or decline, the appearance of a more balanced state between supply and demand is a vital clue that the trend may be about to change.

Figure 1-7c illustrates *umbrella lines*. The concept behind umbrella lines is that the opening and closing prices develop close to the high of the day. The real body, in this case, more closely resembles a square than a rectangle. Umbrellas tend to be bullish after a decline and bearish following an advance. I feel that if they develop during trading ranges, they have no significance.

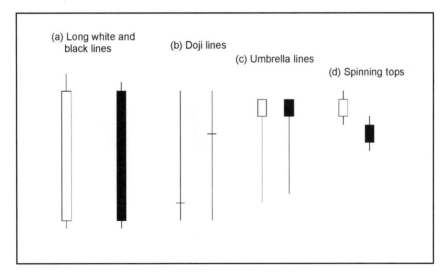

Figure 1-7 Candle variations.

Finally, there are two *spinning tops* (Fig. 1-7d). Small real bodies characterize spinning tops, where the shadows can be short or long. It is the *size of the real body*, rather than the shadow's size, which is important in identifying a spinning top. Spinning tops are not important when they appear in trading ranges, but they do have significance when they develop as part of a price pattern, which represents a battle between the bulls and the bears. In Fig. 1-8 we see another spinning top. Again, the real body is very small, but this time the shadows are long. This candle still qualifies as a spinning top because of the small real body. Figure 1-9 shows another example of a spinning top, this time at a bottom. Spinning tops are the opposite of a long real body, in the sense that long bodies indicate a decisive market where either buyers or sellers are in control. Alternately, spinning tops indicate indecision, where participants cannot agree on whether prices should rally or react. When they develop after a prolonged rally or reaction, they are a sign that upside or downside momentum is dissipating. Putting it in layman's terms, we could say that in previous sessions, buyers or sellers had the upper hand, but the spinning top tells us that the fight is more evenly matched. Thus, another small change in the balance between supply and demand could tip the price trend the other way. This is why a spinning top is an initial sign that a trend may be in the process of reversing. Only when this is confirmed by other price action, which we shall get into later, should you take action.

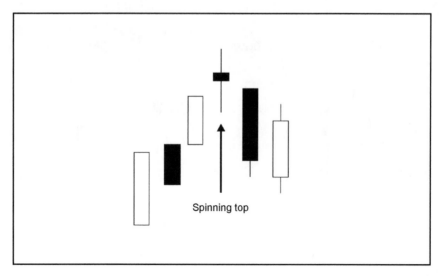

Figure 1-8   Spinning top after a rally.

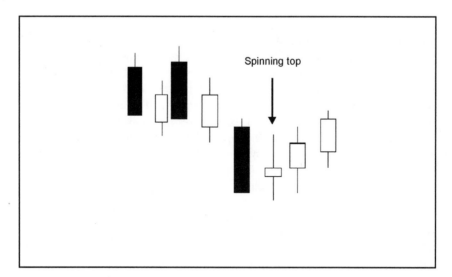

Figure 1-9   Spinning top after a decline.

Spinning Tops and Volume

One other important point concerning spinning tops is their relationship with volume. In a rudimentary way, we can think of accumulation as the process when a security moves from so-called *weak* and *uninformed* people to strong, better-informed ones. One sign of accumulation develops when prices do not move very much but volume is exceedingly heavy. This means that if a spinning top develops after a decline and the volume is extremely heavy, as in Fig. 1-10, this adds further evidence that the trend is probably about to reverse. Note how the volume, represented by the vertical bars, increases tremendously on the day the spinning top with the long shadow is formed.

Distribution occurs at market peaks (Fig. 1-11). The process is exactly the opposite of accumulation, in that the transfer is from strong, informed traders and investors to weak, uninformed ones. Look for a price run-up and a spinning top that is associated with very heavy volume. Once again, the spinning top–heavy volume combination indicates indecision between buyers and sellers. The heavy volume aspect tells us the level of indecision is very high, so when the price confirms by declining, a new downtrend is confirmed.

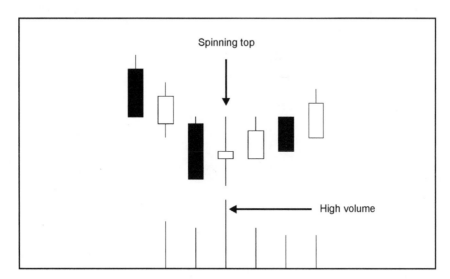

Figure 1-10 Spinning top after a decline showing volume.

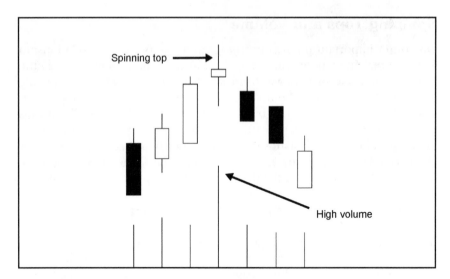

Figure 1-11 Spinning top after an advance showing volume.

Now that we have covered the building blocks, it is time to review some chart patterns. In candles, as with bar charts, there are two types of patterns or formations, reversal and consolidation. We will begin in the next chapter with the reversal variety.

2

Reversal Patterns: I

Hammers and Hanging Men

Hammers and hanging men are 1-day price reversals. Hammers are umbrellas that occur after a price decline, and they get their name because they are said to be *hammering* out a bottom (Fig. 2-1). A hammer is characterized by a day on which prices slip sharply from the opening price during the course of the trading session, then return close to the high of the day.

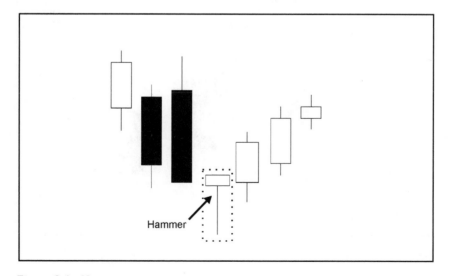

Hammer

Figure 2-1 Hammer.

Hanging men, alternately, are umbrellas that develop after a rally (Fig. 2-2). In a sense, the small real body can be compared to the head of a man, and the long shadow, to his legs dangling down. *The shadow should be at least twice the size of the real body.* Hanging men that develop after a prolonged advance should be treated with great respect, especially if the trading range for the *hanging day* is above the entire trading range of the previous day, as in Fig. 2-3. In bar chart language, the hanging day would be a gap day. The color of either the hanging men or the hammers is not important.

For both types of candles (Fig. 2-4), the necessary characteristics are: first, that the real body should be in the upper end of the trading range, and second, that the long lower shadow is at least twice the height of the real body. Finally, there should be nothing, or very little, in the way of an upper shadow. Generally speaking, these patterns will gain greater significance the longer the lower shadow, the shorter the upper shadow, and the smaller the real body. Hence, the lower shadow should normally be at least twice the size of the real body. Generally, it is much greater. Thus, Fig. 2-5(b) will, other things being equal, be much more significant than Fig. 2-5(a), on the left. Although the color is not too important, a white hammer tends to have more significance than a black one, since it means that the price opens, sells down to the low, and ends on, or very close to, its high. Similarly, a black day tends to be more bearish for a hanging man.

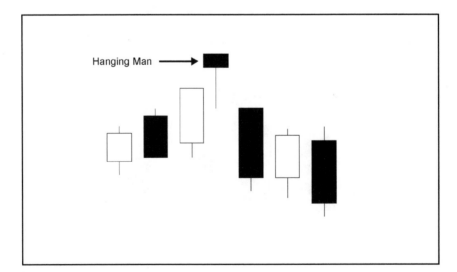

Figure 2-2 Hanging man.

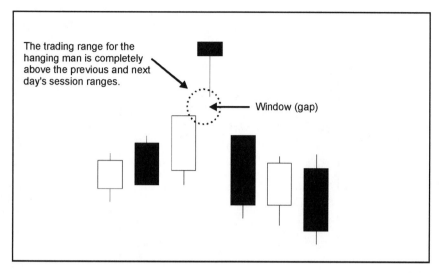

Figure 2-3   Hanging man with window.

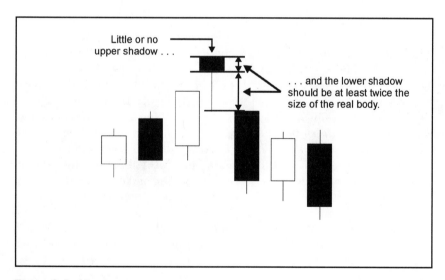

Figure 2-4   Hanging man proportions.

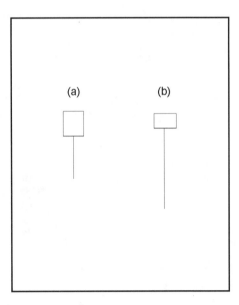

Figure 2-5   Hanging men comparison.

Patterns have bullish and bearish implications, but they usually require some form of confirmation. For example, if a hanging man is followed by a day on which prices trade higher, then the bearish implications of the pattern are partially erased (Fig. 2-6), or, to put it another way, are not confirmed. Alternately, if it is followed by a long black day, the negative implications are confirmed (Fig. 2-7). A generally accepted rule states that *the larger the gap between the opening of the post–hanging man day and the real body of the hanging man, the more likely it is that the hanging man will turn out to be a top.* The rationale is that the opening below the real body means that all those people who bought between the opening and closing price of the hanging day are literally "left hanging." An additional confirmation requirement is for the close of the candle following the hanging day to be comfortably below that of the hanging real body, which it certainly is in Fig. 2-7. It is also important to look at prior price action and other technical factors that we will take a look at when we get to the marketplace examples. Basically, it comes down to the fact that *if prices do not run up prior to a hanging man day, there is nothing to reverse, so there can be no reversal pattern.* The same would be true for a hammer if it is not preceded by a down market.

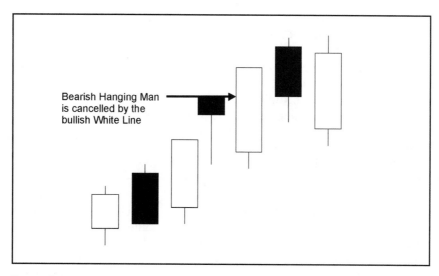

Figure 2-6   Hanging man cancellation.

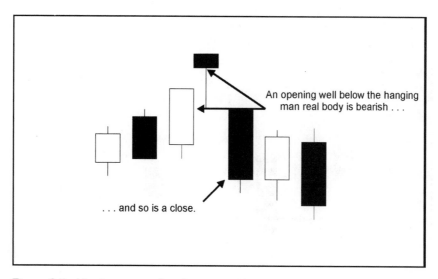

Figure 2-7   Hanging man confirmation.

It might appear at first sight that since the price springs back to close well above the session low and nearer to the high during hanging day, this candle should be bullish. The point seems to be: the very fact the price slips so much during the formation of a hanging man means that the price is vulnerable. If it is then followed in the next session by a weak day, this just confirms that the vulnerability was not a flash in the pan.

In the case of a hammer following a decline, prices slip sharply during the session but close at, or near to, the high. The sell-off represents a bit of a climax. Those who shorted during the session decide to cover, as they find that selling pressure is no longer able to push the price any lower. It is more significant if the lower shadow penetrates an important support area (Fig. 2-8). This is because the violation of the support ought to encourage more people to liquidate long positions or go short. When a break of this nature fails to attract such selling and instead the price rallies toward the high of the day, it indicates the support violation was probably a whipsaw. Since the hammer day, by definition, appears after a prolonged decline, this failed downside-move represents exhaustion. Confirmation will come, the longer the price can hold above the bottom of the lower shadow. Sometimes it experiences a subsequent hammer day, as the bears once again unsuccessfully try to press the market lower. In Fig. 2-8, though, only one hammer day was required, since the price soon took off again on the upside. Since the hammer day represents an emotional extreme, the lower shadow often represents a good point under which to place a stop.

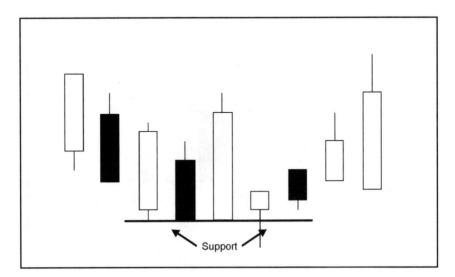

Figure 2-8 Hammer.

Dark Cloud Cover and the Piercing Line

As we all know, dark clouds hint at a coming storm. The dark cloud candlestick formation (Fig. 2-9) does the same thing, but for prices. The pattern consists of two days that follow an advance. The first is a strong, white real body. The second is a black body in which the close occurs in the lower half of the first day's white real body. It is also important for the second day's opening to be higher than the first day's high. You can tell that by making sure the top of the real body is above the first day's upper shadow line. This means that the opening of the second day gaps higher than the trading range of the first day, implying an emotionally bullish opening. However, by the end of the day, the price closes well into the trading range of the prior session, leading to great disappointment among the bulls. In fact, the requirement is that it closes below the halfway point (Fig. 2-10) of the previous real body. Generally speaking, the lower the close on the second day, relative to the real body of the first day, the more bearish the pattern.

Another characteristic that would emphasize the bearishness of one of these formations would develop if the second day opens above a key resistance level and then closes below it (Fig. 2-11). This would then indicate exhaustion, a phenomenon that is usually followed by a sharp decline. The resistance could take the form of an actual level, as in Fig. 2-11, a moving-average crossover, a trendline violation, and so forth. The point is that the

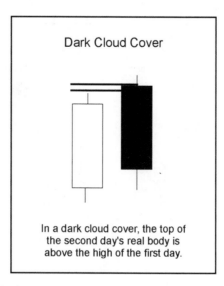

Figure 2-9 Dark cloud cover.

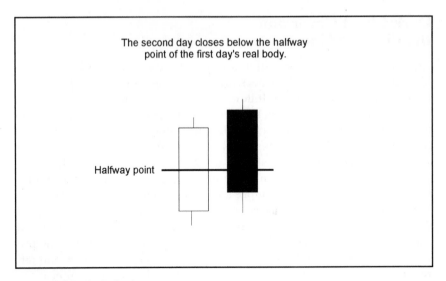

Figure 2-10 Dark cloud cover requirement.

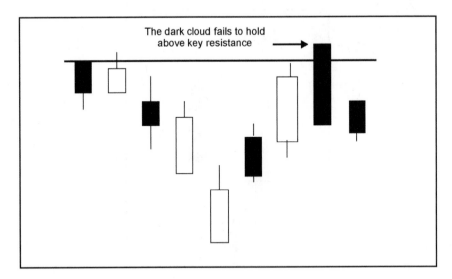

Figure 2-11 Dark cloud cover requirement.

price tries to rally above the resistance and not only fails, but fails convincingly, by forming a dark cloud cover pattern. Another tip-off that a reversal is in the cards develops when the second day is accompanied with very high volume. This is because the greater the level of activity *relative* to the recent past, the greater the significance of the pattern. Finally, if the two candles forming the pattern are both shaven, that is, have very little or no shadows, this increases the odds of the validity of the pattern.

The *piercing line* occurs at market bottoms (Fig. 2-12) and is exactly the opposite to the dark cloud. For this reason, it could more aptly be termed a *sunny sky*. The first day is a strong, black real body, and the second is a white real body that closes in the top half of the first day's real body. The more the price can close above the midpoint, the more positive the implication. Again, it is important for the opening price of the second day to gap completely beyond the first day's real body, as shown in Fig. 2-12. The principles determining the significance of dark clouds apply to piercing lines, but in reverse. Thus, if the second day opens below a major support level (Fig. 2-13) and then meets the other qualifications of this pattern, it indicates downside exhaustion. Also, if the second day is accompanied by exceptionally heavy volume, this suggests a form of selling climax. One thing to bear in mind with the piercing line versus the dark cloud is the fact it is more important for the second day to close well into the top half of the first. It would appear that prices can fall from their own weight but require stronger momentum to rally.

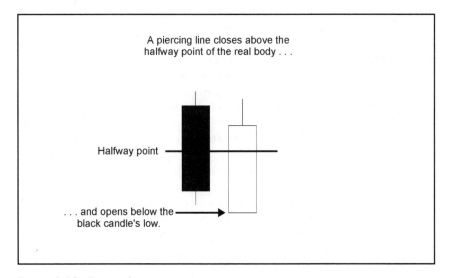

Figure 2-12 Piercing line.

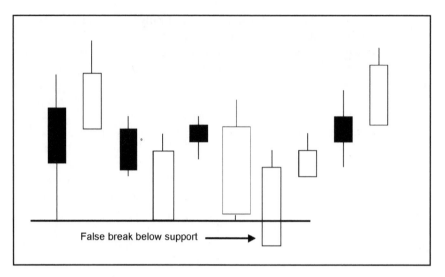

Figure 2-13 Piercing line.

Engulfing Patterns

Engulfing patterns (Figs. 2-14 and 2-15) are 2-day affairs and are similar to the dark cloud and piercing line formations. The principal difference is that the second day for a bearish engulfing pattern not only closes more than halfway along the first day's white real body but below it, thereby "engulfing" it. A bearish engulfing pattern develops after a rally. The first day consists of a long white real body, followed by a dark real body, whose opening price is higher than the first day's close and whose closing price is also below the first day's open. Though the second real body should engulf the first, it is immaterial whether it also engulfs the shadows. Both days in an engulfing pattern should be relatively shadowless. This is an important difference from the dark cloud–piercing line formations since the real body of the second day should engulf the extreme shadow of the preceding session. In the case of a dark cloud, the extreme shadow would be the upper one, and in the case of a piercing line, it would be the lower one.

A bullish engulfing pattern (Fig. 2-15) is the exact opposite of the bearish one. This formation, which follows a decline, consists of a long, black real body followed by a long, white real body, which engulfs the first day's body. It is the second day that gives us a clue as to the psychology underlying the pattern because the price opens on, or close to, the low, as people expect the bearish action of the previous days to continue. Then, as the session proceeds, the bears lose their enthusiasm and prices close up on the

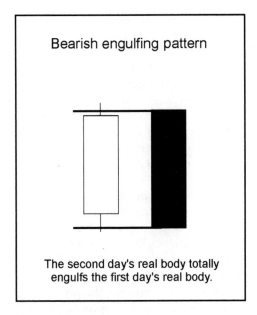

Figure 2-14 Bearish engulfing pattern.

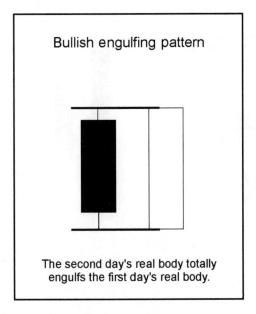

Figure 2-15 Bullish engulfing pattern.

day. This 1-day reversal of downside to upside momentum is sufficiently great to result in a change in sentiment and, therefore, in trend.

There are several characteristics that enhance the significance of an engulfing pattern. First, generally speaking, the longer and sharper the trend preceding the pattern, the greater its significance (Fig. 2-16). For example, a bearish engulfing pattern developing after a small price advance will have less validity than one following a more lengthy rally, because a pattern that forms after a sharp price move is more subject to profit-taking.

The opposite would be true in a downtrend, where an engulfing pattern following a sharp sell-off is more likely to be followed by a reversal than one after a shallow decline.

Second, unusually heavy volume on the second day is indicative of exhaustion. It is possible, for example, that after a decline, heavy volume on the second day indicates a small selling climax. Traders come into the day selling heavily, as they believe prices will decline. Then, when they do not, the selling is exhausted and sentiment moves in favor of the buyers.

Third, the larger the second day's real body relative to the initial day, the more likely that sentiment and, therefore, the previous trend has changed. In Fig. 2-17, we see two different engulfing tops. The one on the left (a) is the stronger of the two because its real body engulfs both the shadows and

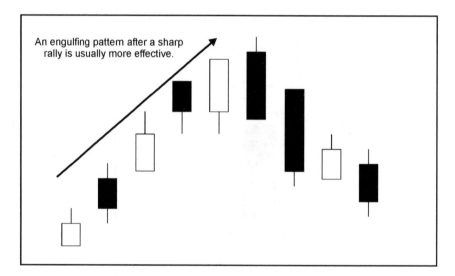

Figure 2-16 Engulfing pattern.

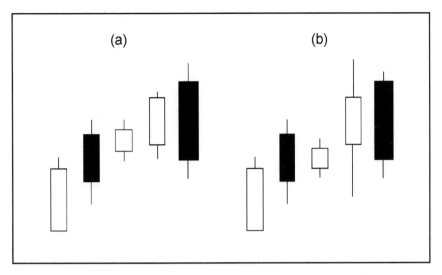

Figure 2-17   Bearish engulfing pattern.

the real body of its predecessor. The one on the right (b) is still a valid pattern, but has less strength, due to the fact the real body of the engulfing day only engulfs the real body of the day before. In effect, the change in psychology is much more pronounced, the more engulfing the engulfing candle can achieve.

Taken a step further, if the second day engulfs more than just the first day of the pattern, an even stronger signal of a change in sentiment is given. In Fig. 2-18, we see two engulfing days: one for a top on the left (Fig. 2-18a), and another for a bottom on the right (Fig. 2-18b). Note that the second day of both formations not only engulfs the previous session, but several others, as well. This is a stronger signal, since the engulfed days really represent an extended period in which buyers and sellers are rather well matched. The engulfing day tips the balance decisively in one direction or the other.

It is also possible to have an engulfing day in which the second candle has an identical opening to the first's close (Fig. 2-19). An example of a top is shown on the left and one for a bottom on the right. In a strict technical sense, the second candle does not truly engulf the first, but it is surprising how potent this variation can be.

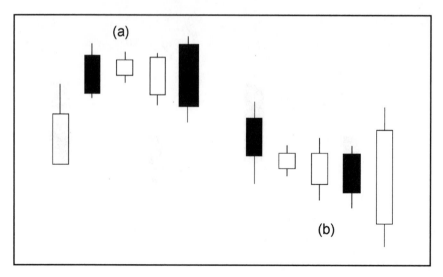

Figure 2-18   Engulfing several days.

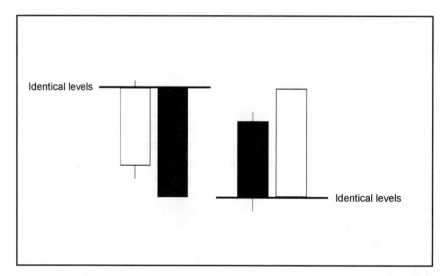

Figure 2-19   Engulfing pattern variations.

The "Last" Engulfing Pattern

Bearish engulfing patterns develop after an advance. However, if they appear after a decline, they are called a *last engulfing bottom* (Fig. 2-20). This is because it is actually a bullish pattern. The formation is identical to the bearish engulfing pattern we saw earlier, since it consists of a small white day being engulfed by a long black one. However, *to be a positive market force, it must be confirmed by a close above the black candle's close.*

The same phenomenon can be observed in reverse (Fig. 2-21) in a market in which a small black day is engulfed by a long white one. Confirmation in the form of a close below the previous session's white candle close is also required. This pattern is then known as a *last engulfing day top.*

Both types of "last" patterns do not have the kind of outcome one might normally expect, since a long black candle has bearish overtones and a long white one is typically a positive sign. Just bear in mind that the last engulfing pattern comes after a trend has been underway for a while. The long white day indicates a positive attitude among market participants, as they override the small preceding black day. However, the failure of prices to follow through on this new-found bullishness means there has been a change in psychology, and the trend reverses to a bearish one.

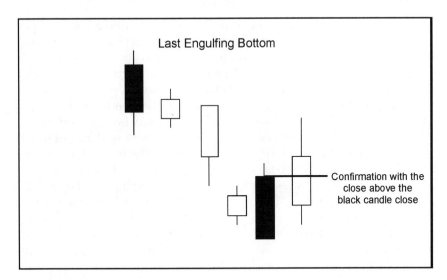

Figure 2-20   Last engulfing bottom.

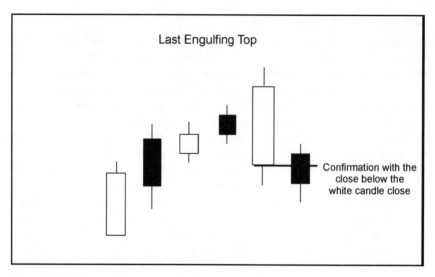

Figure 2-21 Last engulfing top.

Stars

Stars are a combination of long real bodies and spinning tops, or, put another way, a star consists of a small real body that gaps away from a long real body. Their color is not important. In each case, the quiet action indicated by the small real body indicates a balance between supply and demand. If a star appears after a relatively protracted rally or reaction, it indicates that the previously prevailing bullish or bearish forces no longer have the upper hand, so a possible trend reversal may be in the offing.

Stars come in four principal varieties: morning, evening, doji, and shooting. Let us begin with the morning star (Fig. 2-22). The morning star is said to begin a new day of hope and is, therefore, bullish. These patterns are formed with two long real bodies separated by a spinning top. Figure 2-22 only shows the first two candles. The actual star is the spinning top, which is made with a gap. In this case, the real body of the star falls outside the range of the other two real bodies (Fig. 2-23). It is also possible for the star to open a window (gap) by falling completely outside of the entire trading range of the previous black candle.

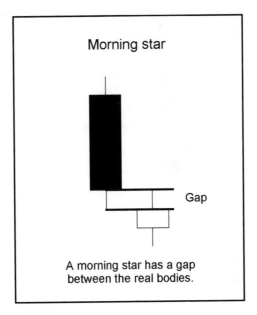

Figure 2-22   Morning star.

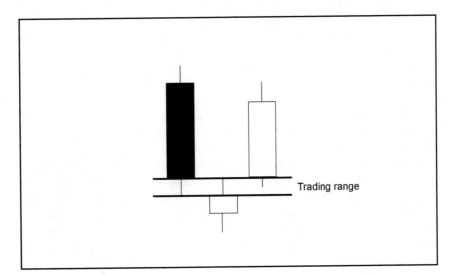

Figure 2-23   Morning star.

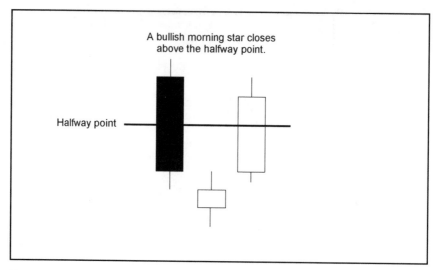

A bullish morning star closes
above the halfway point.

Halfway point

Figure 2-24 Morning star.

The first real body should be black. The color of the star is not important because it reflects a balance between buyers and sellers following a strong trend where sellers have dominated. The color of the third day is important, for if it is to signal a reversal from seller to buyer dominance, it should reflect this with a white candle. It should also close above the halfway point of the first real body as shown in Fig. 2-24. The more it can close into the first day's real body, the stronger the effect.

The evening star (Fig. 2-25) is the reverse of the morning star. It, too, consists of three days. A long white body, separated from a black real body by a spinning top. The real body of the spinning top should also fall outside the real body of the first day (Fig. 2-26), even better if there is a gap on both sides of the star. Finally, the third day should close more than halfway below the midpoint of the first (Fig. 2-27), that is, below the horizontal line.

Technicians usually like to see a confirmation of the star. In the case of a top, this would take the form of a long, dark real body. If a long, white real body follows, the odds are greater that the pattern will fail. Finally, heavier volume on the third day of the pattern will increase its significance. In the case of a morning star (Figs. 2-28 and 2-29), the previous trend is negative and it is normal in a declining trend for volume to contract. It is also a bearish sign when volume declines on a rally. Therefore, rising volume on the third day is not characteristic of a declining trend and would enhance the bullish implications of the pattern.

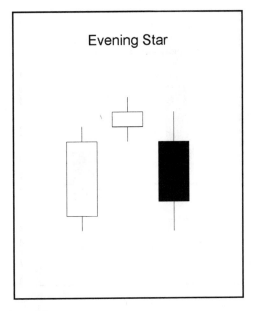

Figure 2-25   Evening star.

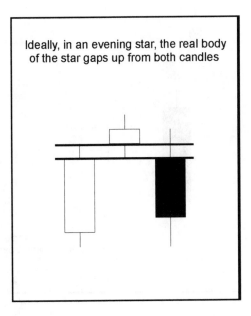

Figure 2-26   Evening star.

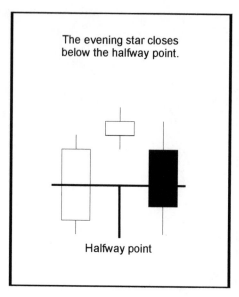

Figure 2-27 Evening star.

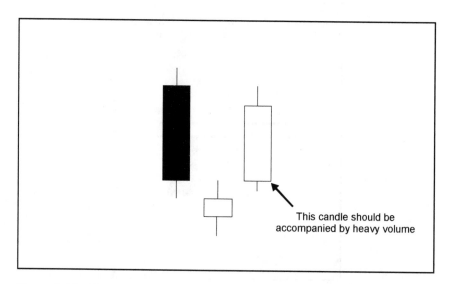

Figure 2-28 Morning star.

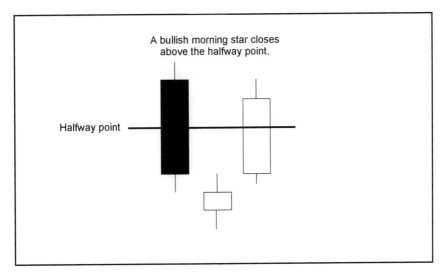

Figure 2-29 Morning star.

In the case of an evening star, the expanding volume on the third day, which is down, would be abnormal, since volume normally goes with the trend, that is, contracts on declines and expands on rallies. When volume expands on a decline, unless this is a selling climax, it is invariably a negative sign.

Doji Stars

A doji star consists of a long real body followed by a *small* doji (Fig. 2-30). You may recall that a doji is a day on which the opening and closing prices are more or less identical. A doji star offers a warning that a trend is about to reverse. The long real body should be colored in the direction of the then-prevailing trend. In other words, if the prevailing trend is up, look for a white real body. If the prevailing trend is down, look for a dark real body for the first day, as in the example on the right of Fig. 2-30. The doji should gap outside of the first day's real body. Note that the trading range for the doji day is very small. The real body on the third day should be the opposite color to the first. In other words, an evening doji star, as shown on the left hand side of Fig. 2-30, would have a black real body on the third day and a morning doji star would have a white one.

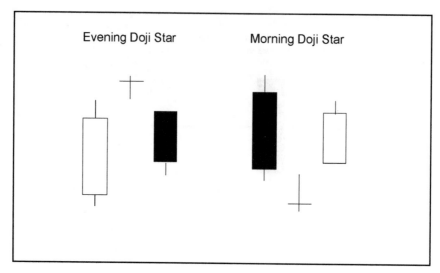

Figure 2-30   Doji stars.

The same rules of significance relating to third-day volume and the third-day closing discussed for regular morning and evening stars, also apply to the doji variety (Fig. 2-31). In other words, for reversals of downtrends, look for heavy volume on the third day and for a closing that develops above the halfway point of the first candle (Fig. 2-32). Third-day tops are emphasized when they are associated with heavy volume. The third day should also close well into the lower half of the first day's real body. Other things being equal, the doji stars are more significant than regular morning and evening stars. This is because their narrower real bodies represent a finer balance between buyers and sellers. Consequently, when this battle is resolved, the signal is much stronger.

There is one other point concerning significance, and that is, if the doji day is completely separated from the other two candles (in other words, forms a kind of island where not even the shadows overlap), this is a much stronger signal than if the shadows overlap. In Western chart language we would call this a *1-day island reversal,* since the entire trading range forms a kind of island (Fig. 2-33). The official candlestick terminology for such a day is an *abandoned baby.* While abandoned children appear at both tops and bottoms, they are fairly rare phenomena. In Fig. 2-33 we see two abandoned

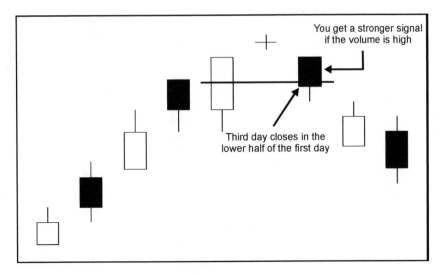

Figure 2-31   Evening doji star.

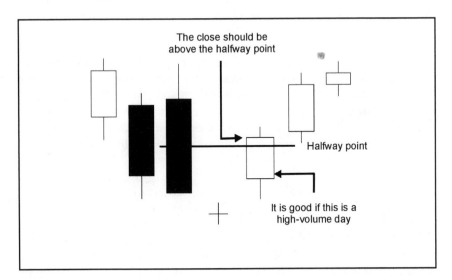

Figure 2-32   Morning doji star.

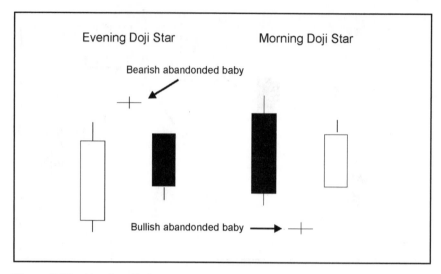

Figure 2-33 Abandoned babies.

babies, one at a top on the left and the other at a market bottom. Notice how the "baby" is totally separated from the two lower shadows on either side.

One hint that a doji star may not be "working" occurs when, during a downtrend, the third candle gaps below the doji and the color of this candle is black (Fig. 2-34). In such instances, the bullish implication from the doji is invalidated. The opposite would be true for a top (Fig. 2-35) in that the third candle gaps up from the doji day and the color of that candle is white. Once a doji has been spotted, it is equally important to wait for the third and fourth days to make sure they confirm the bullish implications of a morning doji and bearish ones for an evening variety.

Shooting Stars and Inverted Hammers

Finally, we turn to the shooting star (Fig. 2-36). This is a short-term top where, after an advance, the price action usually creates a small gap, and a small real body appears at the lower end of a long wick, or upper shadow. In a sense, it is a kind of reverse-hanging-man. The color of the star is not

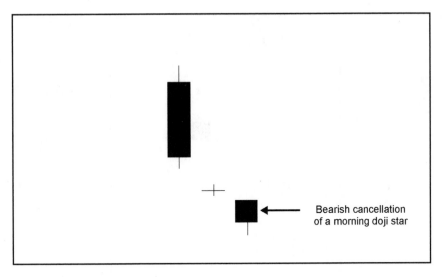

Figure 2-34   Doji star cancellation.

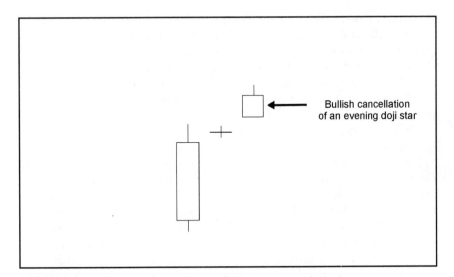

Figure 2-35   Doji star cancellation.

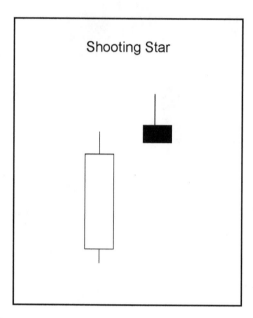

Figure 2-36 Shooting star.

important, though the presence of a good gap emphasizes the significance of the candle. A shooting star indicates the price opens close to the low, then rallies in an impressive way. However, the rally falters and prices end the session at, or close to, their opening level, depending on the color of the real body. It is a disappointing day, since the higher prices during the middle of the day are not sustained, and all those traders who bought during this period go home with a loss.

When a shooting star appears after a price decline, it is known as an *inverted hammer*, because that is what it really is. The formation is the same as the shooting star; however, because it appears after a decline, its implications are bullish (Fig. 2-37). The key, once again, is the small real body compared to the long shadow. The color of the inverted hammer is immaterial. It is a bullish candle, but it is of paramount importance to wait for some confirmation in subsequent sessions. This could take the form of a white candle with a higher opening the next day, that is, where the real body gaps up from the inverted hammer's real body. Generally speaking, the wider the gap, the stronger the confirmation. If this candle also turns out to be a long, white real body, so much the better. Usually, the longer the price is able to hold above the real body of the inverted hammer, the greater the odds that a bottom has been formed. On the face of it, the inverted ham-

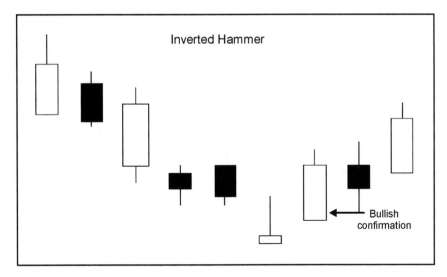

Figure 2-37   Inverted hammer.

mer day looks bearish, since the bulls are unable to sustain the rally and prices close near their low for the session; therefore, confirmation is important. Obviously, there are a lot of traders who look at this action and then go short. Consequently, if on the day of the confirmation, the price opens higher and then continues to rally, events are not working out the way the shorts anticipated, so they cover and add fuel to the rally. It is not so much that the inverted hammer is bullish, it is more the combination of a bearish scenario that is invalidated by the bullish confirmation.

More on Dojis

You may recall that a doji is a candle in which the opening and closing prices are more or less identical. The example in Fig. 2-38 is known as a *long-legged doji*. In a way, it indicates indecision, since prices fluctuate greatly throughout the day, as can be appreciated from the long shadows. However, at the end of the day, the price returns to its opening level. The long-legged doji, therefore, has no forecasting value, except to say that when it appears after a sustained rally or reaction, it indicates a closer balance between buyers and sellers, compared to the previous sessions when one or the other was clearly in command. Therefore, be on the lookout for confirmation of a reversal in the subsequent candles. Figure 2-39 features a top reversal. Note

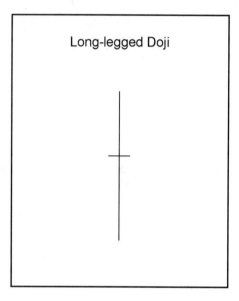

Figure 2-38 Long-legged doji.

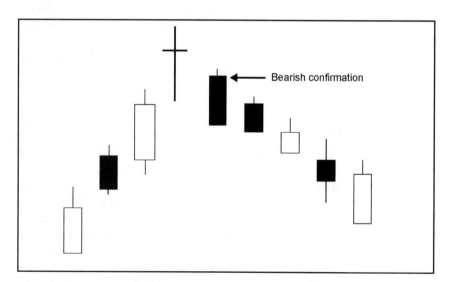

Figure 2-39 Long-legged doji.

how the black candle following the long-legged doji opens below the doji and closes well into the real body of the white candle that preceded it.

Alternately, the gravestone doji (Fig. 2-40) shows the opening and closing prices occurring at the low for the day and is quite bearish. We typically see it at the end of an advance, where the upper shadow represents new high ground for the move (Fig. 2-41). The fact that prices end the day at the opening (after all that work at higher levels) is indicative of a change in psychology and is really a sign of exhaustion. In this case, the longer the shadow, the more negative the omen. In the strictest sense, a doji ends the session at the same price it began. However, a more lenient interpretation would allow some leeway, in that the opening and closing prices, though not exactly identical, are still extremely close together. The distinction is quite subtle. When bending the interpretation, always bear in mind the basic underlying psychology that a doji is trying to reflect: a session that ends up in indecision. What constitutes the difference between a liberally interpreted gravestone doji and a shooting star with an extremely small real body and unusually long upper shadow can be a mute point. However, the effect of both types of candles is very similar. Basically, the closer the opening and closing prices, the more powerful the omen.

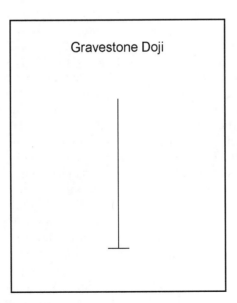

Figure 2-40 Gravestone doji.

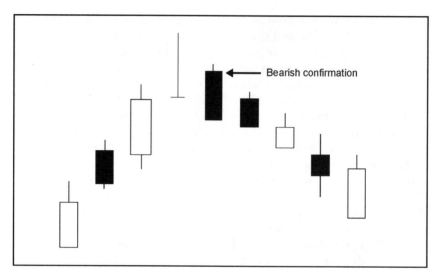

Figure 2-41   Gravestone doji.

This principle applies to all forms of doji and is not limited to the grave-stone variety. Another way to judge how wide a tolerance, if any, should be given to the difference between the opening and closing prices is to relate the doji to previous candles. If they have small real bodies, then go for a very strict doji definition. In Fig. 2-42, we see three very small real bodies, so there is no room for any differential between the open and close. On the other hand, in Fig. 2-43, they have particularly long real bodies. This allows a little more latitude. You can see that the doji is represented by a thick line. In this instance, the integrity of the idea that supply and demand are in balance has not been violated because, proportionate to the previous sessions' trading ranges, the open and close of the "doji" day are relatively close.

The dragonfly doji (Fig. 2-44) represents a more optimistic scenario. This is really a special case of the hammer that we looked at earlier. The psychology is the exact reverse of the gravestone doji. These candles should develop at the end of a decline. The price should open at the high, then sell off (the more the merrier, in this case), finally rallying back to the opening levels at the high for the day.

A doji that appears after a long white candle (Fig. 2-45) is especially ominous. This is because a long white candle indicates the buyers are in solid control. The doji, alternately, indicates that an important shift may be under-way, since the doji day represents one in which both forces are more or less

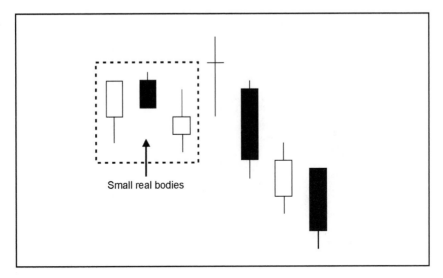

Figure 2-42 Doji comparing previous real body sizes.

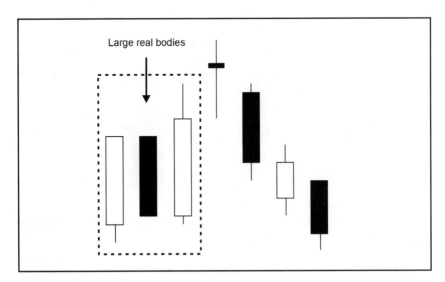

Figure 2-43 Doji comparing previous real body sizes.

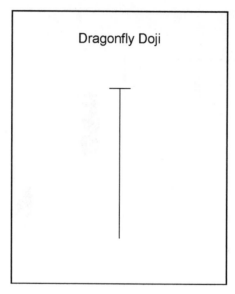

Figure 2-44   Dragonfly doji.

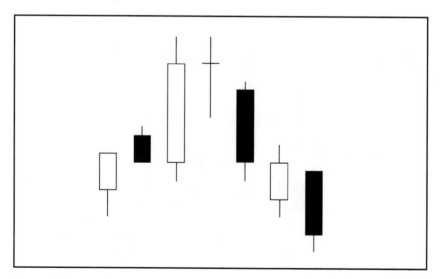

Figure 2-45   Doji following a long white day.

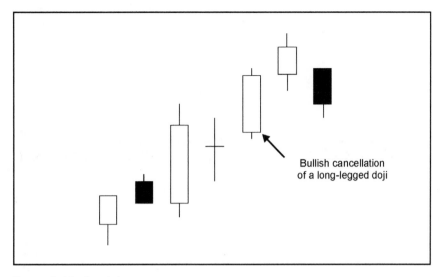

Figure 2-46 Doji failure.

equally matched. In this respect, it does not matter whether the doji appears within the range of the prior day's real body or not, because the very presence of the doji indicates a loss of upside momentum. The same principle, but in reverse, applies to doji that appears next to a long black day after a decline has taken place.

As discussed earlier, a doji merely points out that there is balance between buyers and sellers. It marks a caution flag on the field so far as the current trend is concerned and must be confirmed. If it is not, and the price moves higher (as in Fig. 2-46), then the balance is once again resolved in favor of the buyers. Here the doji appears after a long white day. At this point, it would have looked as though the trend was about to reverse. However, the next candle was a relatively long white day, which took the price higher. This, in effect, told us that the stand-off between demand and supply as reflected in the doji had been resolved, only this time in favor of the buyers. The appropriate place to have placed any short stop would have been above the high of the doji day. Remember, *a regular doji by itself is not sufficient evidence to take action,* so this is a fine example of why waiting for confirmation of a trend change is an insurance policy worth paying.

3
Reversal Patterns: II

Upside-Gap Two Crows

The *upside-gap two crows* occurs after a rally (Fig. 3-1). It consists of a long, white real body followed by two small, black real bodies, the crows. The first black real body gaps up from the white body. In other words, its real body is totally above that of the first day (Fig. 3-2). This is where the *upside-gap* in the name of this pattern comes from. The second black real body normally closes the window (gap); however, because it is a black day, the implication is bearish. Ideally, the real body of this third day of the pattern should engulf the second day, yet still close above the close of the first day (Fig. 3-3). The pattern gets its name from the idea that the two black candlesticks represent two black crows looking down from a tree. Just remember, *the gaps are caused by the real bodies:* in this case, *an overlap by the shadows is quite acceptable.* Also, the two crows do not have to be small. Either of them can be a longish black body; though, to qualify, the second crow must, of course, engulf the first, as shown in Fig. 3-4.

The rationale behind this pattern is that the first *crow* day opens substantially higher than the previous day, hence, the gap in the real body. Then the price closes below the open. Sentiment remains optimistic because this close is still above the previous session. On the third day, prices again open sharply higher but actually close down on the day. The pattern, therefore, indicates there is little in the way of upside momentum because the price cannot hold its gains. Worse still, it actually closes on a weak note. This disappointing action discourages the bulls, who then begin to question why

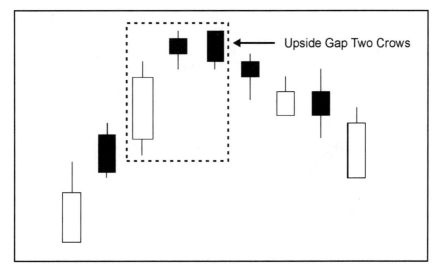

Figure 3-1 Upside-gap two crows.

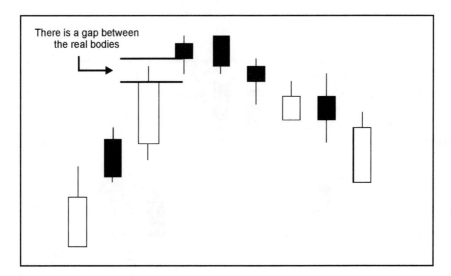

Figure 3-2 Upside-gap two crows gapping requirement.

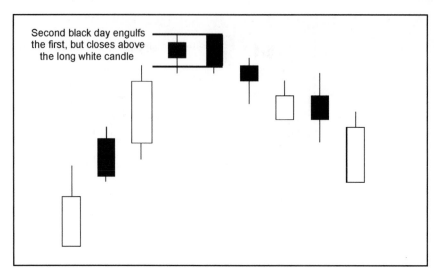

Figure 3-3   Upside-gap two crows engulfing requirement.

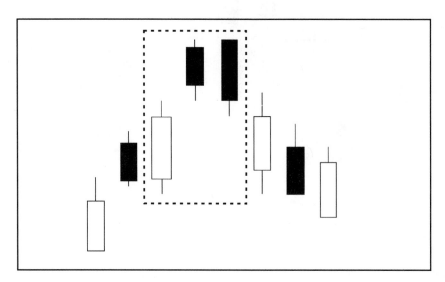

Figure 3-4   Upside-gap two crows variation.

there was no upside follow-through. Consequently, they start to liquidate the next day and the price retreats. As you can appreciate, this formation is really a variation on the engulfing pattern, since the second crow engulfs the first.

As with all candlestick patterns, it is best to wait for a confirmation, which should take the form of a black candlestick that closes lower than the second crow.

Three Black Crows

The *three black crows* pattern (Fig. 3-5) consists of three declining black candlesticks that form after an advance. They indicate lower prices. Each candle should close at, or close to, its session low (Fig. 3-6) which means that none of the candles have much, if any, of a lower wick. A final characteristic is that each of the three real bodies opens within the range of the previous session's real body.

A rare but especially bearish variety is the *identical three crows* formation (Fig. 3-7). This develops when the openings of the second and third crows are identical, or extremely close, to the close of the previous session. You can see in Fig. 3-7 that there is no respite from the downtrend as each opening price touches the closing price of its predecessor. This pattern is quite rare, but deserves respect because it has the reputation of being an especially negative one.

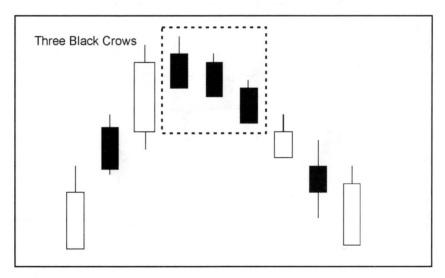

Figure 3-5   Three black crows.

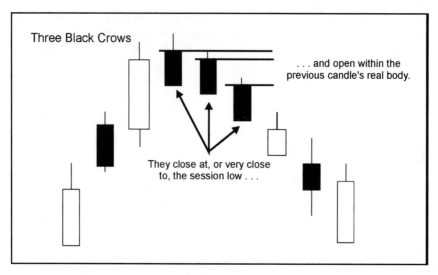

Figure 3-6   Three black crows opening and closing requirement.

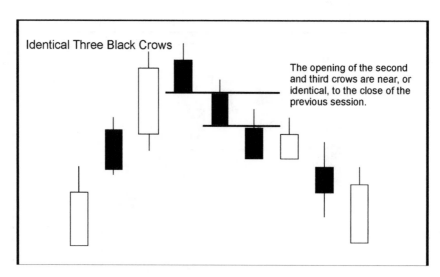

Figure 3-7   Identical three black crows.

Harami Formations

A *harami* (Fig. 3-8) consists of two candles. The real body of the second is totally engulfed by the first. *Harami* is an old Japanese word for pregnant, and the second candle corresponds to the fetus of a pregnant woman. It is the opposite of an engulfing pattern, except that in an engulfing pattern, the two candles are of different colors and the engulfing is done on the first, not the second, day. For a harami it is better, though not a prerequisite, for the candles to be of differing colors. However, after an advance, it is even better (from the point of view of a reliable signal) to see two black candles. After a decline, the best combination is white, as shown in Fig. 3-9. Normally, the harami will be the same as a Western inside day, but whereas the inside day will be totally encompassed by the trading range of the previous session, for a harami, it is the real body that must be on the inside of the previous session.

As a general rule, the smaller the real body relative to the previous candle, the more significant the pattern. This is because the second day is one of indecision following a sharp, emotionally charged price move, as reflected in the first, longer candle day. Consequently, the second day of the harami indicates there is no follow-through, and a trend reversal may be in the wind.

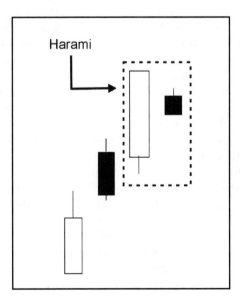

Figure 3-8 Harami.

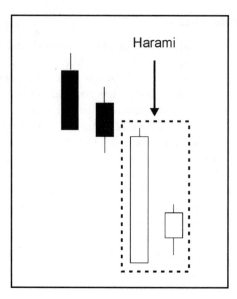

Figure 3-9   Harami.

It is a day in a declining market when market participants say to each other, "Well, we have had the sell-off, are prices not cheap enough now or have all the speculative longs been taken out?" and so on. The point is that before the sell-off, they were confident of a decline. Now, on the second day of the harami, some doubt has crept in.

When the second day is a doji, the pattern is known as a *harami cross* (Fig. 3-10). Since dojis are relatively significant candles, a harami cross is normally a stronger pattern than a straight harami. Also, since the opening and closing prices are either identical, or very close, to one another, this increases the indecision and, therefore, its importance. While the shadows can extend beyond the previous session, a necessary feature of the harami cross is a very small real body relative to the previous candle. If a harami cross appears after a relatively strong price move, the indecisive action of the doji day indicates that the previous upside or downside momentum has dissipated. Consequently, a change in trend may be expected. The very fact that the price opens and closes at approximately the same level tells us there is a certain amount of indecision between buyers and sellers.

Generally speaking, if during a rally, a harami or doji cross develops toward the upper end of a long candle (Fig. 3-11), then the possibilities of consolidation, as opposed to a trend reversal, are increased. The reverse

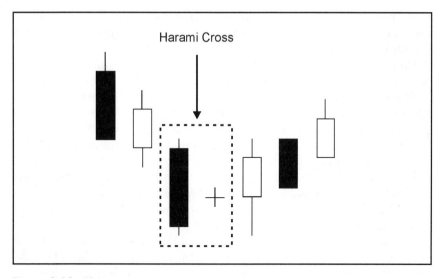

Figure 3-10   Harami cross.

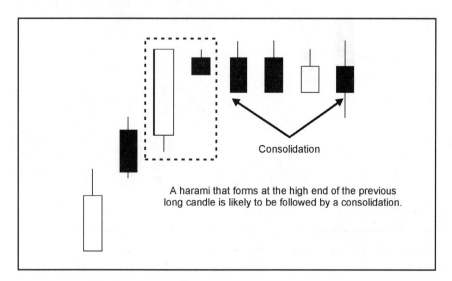

Figure 3-11   High-end harami at a top.

would be true (Fig. 3-12) in a downtrend where a harami that forms at the lower end of the first day's long candle is more likely to be followed by a consolidation.

Alternately, if it forms at the lower end of a long candle following a bull trend, this increases the odds that the harami is a reversal pattern. In a downtrend, a harami may form near the top of a long white body formed by the previous candle. Such action is often a signal the indecision flagged by the harami is going to be resolved in a positive way (Fig. 3-13).

Haramis are pretty common formations and as such are not as reliable as, say, engulfing patterns. However, if the second day is totally confined within the first, including the upper and lower shadows, then it is more likely to be reliable. Also, a doji has more significance than a second candle with a small real body. Finally, the shorter the shadows and the smaller the real body of the second day, the stronger the signal.

One other important aspect is that a harami that follows a sharp advance or decline is more likely to offer a valid and stronger signal. This is because sharp price movements indicate that either buyers or sellers are strongly in control. Since the harami is a signal of balance, it offers a more vivid contrast in the change of sentiment when following a sharp price movement.

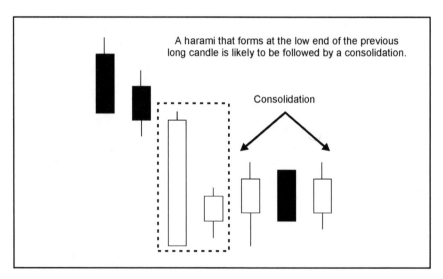

Figure 3-12   Low-end harami at a bottom.

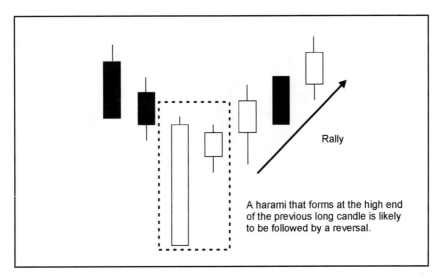

Rally

A harami that forms at the high end
of the previous long candle is likely
to be followed by a reversal.

Figure 3-13   High end harami at a bottom.

Tweezer Tops and Bottoms

If you hold a tweezer upside down, you will see that the two points are of
identical levels (Fig. 3-14). The same is true of a tweezer top, which consists
of two candles for which the highs for the day are identical. Actually, it is
possible for a tweezer to consist of more than two days with an identical top.
Make no mistake about it: we are talking about the high, which can be a
shadow or real-body close or open. This is a short-term bearish pattern
because the first day's high acts as resistance. Consequently, when the second day is unable to punch through the horizontal line that marks the area
of the top, it indicates a loss of upside momentum. If the second tweezer
day also engulfs the first's real body, this emphasizes the strength of the pattern.

Tweezer bottoms occur when, after a decline, two or more candles make
an identical low. This again indicates a loss of downside momentum, since
the price finds support in the area of the low. Figure 3-14 shows a tweezer
literally hammered out because the second low to touch the horizontal line
is a part of a hammer candle.

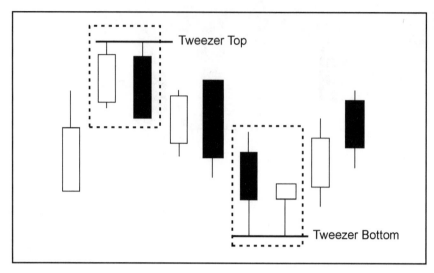

Figure 3-14 Tweezer top and bottom.

Generally speaking, tweezers are not that significant a pattern, but their importance is increased when the level of support at a bottom, or resistance at a top, is strong. For example, after an extended move, a normal market will show signs of exhaustion quicker than if a price trend is unfolding at a more leisurely pace. Just think of a person trying to jump over a hurdle. It will be much more difficult if he has just run a marathon than if he approaches the hurdle after a short jog. The same is true of markets. If the price runs into resistance after a sharp run-up, that resistance (other things being equal) is likely to be far more formidable as a barrier than if the trend has just gotten underway.

The second factor that will increase the significance of a tweezer is the nature of the pattern being formed. For example, if the second day of a tweezer top is a hanging man, as in Fig. 3-15, we have two pieces of evidence that the trend may be about to reverse: the tweezer and the hanging man. Alternately, the second day might be a doji, so the tweezer would really be a harami cross. It could also be a shooting star.

Alternatively, a tweezer bottom may also be a morning star, harami, harami cross, hammer, and so forth.

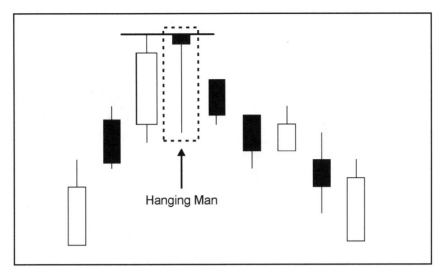

Figure 3-15 Tweezer top (hanging man).

Belt-Hold Lines

A bullish *belt-hold* (Fig. 3-16) is a one-candle pattern consisting of a long candle in which the price opens on the session low and then works its way higher throughout the session. The price does not have to close at the high, but the longer the real body, the more positive the candle. Also, if a belt-hold has not appeared on the chart for quite a while, it becomes an unusual phenomenon which enhances its importance. This is because traders are making a very strong statement about their feelings toward the market with a belt-hold, compared to the smaller candles that were previously the norm. Just think of a crowd murmuring, then a loud voice coming from within the crowd. It is obviously a person who wants to be heard. The belt-hold following a long period of smaller candles amounts to the same thing. It is a one-day pattern that says loudly, "Listen to me because I am telling you the short-term trend has changed."

A bearish belt-hold (Fig. 3-17) is the opposite. It is a long black candle in which the price opens at the high and then works its way lower as the session progresses. Because belt-holds form with little or no shadow at the open they are sometimes called *white* or *black opening shaven heads*. Sometimes these one-day formations are cancelled with a close below the opening of a white belt-hold or one above the opening of a black belt-hold.

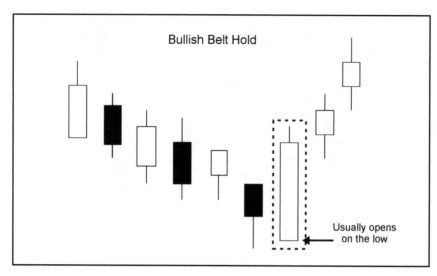

Figure 3-16   Bullish belt-hold.

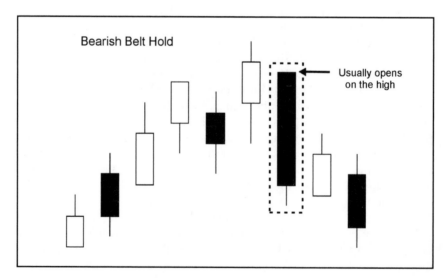

Figure 3-17   Bearish belt-hold.

Belt-holds are often important pivotal days since the high and low occasionally act as support and resistance areas in subsequent price action. The halfway point of the real body of a belt-hold also should be monitored for a possible price reversal during later price swings.

Counterattack or Meeting Lines

A bullish *counterattack line* (Fig. 3-18) develops when, after a decline, a black candle is followed by a white candle and both close or "meet" at the same level. This is why this two-day pattern is sometimes referred to as a *meeting line*. The first day is usually a long black candle. The second day opens sharply lower, leading most traders to believe prices will continue to give way. However, by the end of the day, the price has regained everything lost (a counterattack by the buyers) and closes unchanged. The meeting line, therefore, indicates that the downside momentum has probably dissipated and a reversal in trend is likely.

A bearish counterattack or meeting line (Fig. 3-19), is formed when, after an advance, a white candle is followed by a black candle and both close at the same level. The psychology behind this one is fairly evident. The sharply

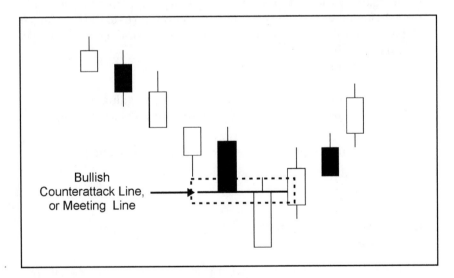

Figure 3-18 Bullish counterattack (meeting) line.

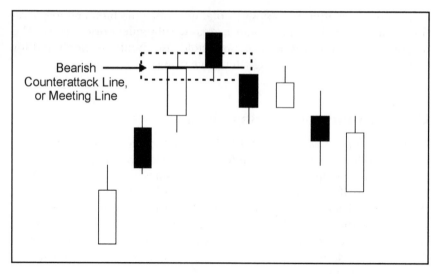

Figure 3-19   Bearish counterattack (meeting) line.

higher opening on the second day has the bulls in a euphoric mood, since these new gains come on top of an already sharp rally. However, euphoria turns to disappointment as the price unexpectedly returns to the unchanged level. Perhaps for the first time in several sessions, the price closes on a weak note, indicating the possibility of a short-term reversal.

More specific rules for identifying these patterns are:

a) The first day is colored in the direction of the prevailing trend and the second day forms in the opposite color (white/black for tops and black/white for bottoms).

b) Both real bodies extend the prevailing trend and are long.

c) The closes are identical.

Three Mountains and Three Rivers

Three mountains and *three rivers* are larger than any pattern so far considered and are generally more significant. The three mountains correspond to the western triple top and consist of three rallies that find resistance at more or less the same level. The third peak should ideally contain a bearish candlestick pattern, such as an engulfing or dark cloud formation, and so on.

If the central peak is higher than the other two, this is known as the *three buddhas* and can be compared to our own head-and-shoulders formations. A three–buddhas pattern is shown in Chart 3-1 of General Motors. The concept comes from the fact that in Buddhist temples there are three Buddhas. The largest is in the middle with two smaller ones on either side. Confirmation for these formations occurs when the price falls below the line joining the two reaction lows separating the three peaks, ideally on a black candle day. In Chart 3-2, we see the buddha, or "head" as we would say in western analysis, toping out with an engulfing pattern. A small engulfing formation is also present on the right buddha.

The equivalent bottom for the mountain and buddha tops are the *three river bottom* and *inverted buddhas* (Chart 3-3). They again are similar to the western triple bottom and inverted head-and-shoulder patterns. It is good if the third bottom should be associated with a bullish candlestick pattern, such as a piercing line, a bullish engulfing pattern, and so on. Confirmation occurs when the price rallies above the trendline joining the two rally peaks. This should develop on a white candle day. In Chart 3-3, we see the breakout take place between two long white candles. Note the top of the left inverted buddha is signaled with a very strong engulfing day.

Chart 3-1 General Motors and three buddhas. (Source: *pring.com*)

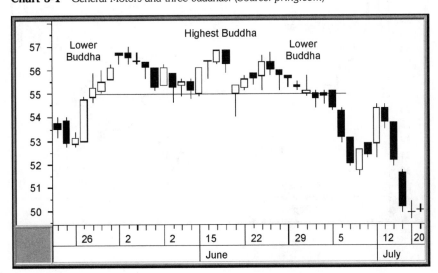

Chart 3-2 General Motors and a three-buddha top. (Source: *pring.com*)

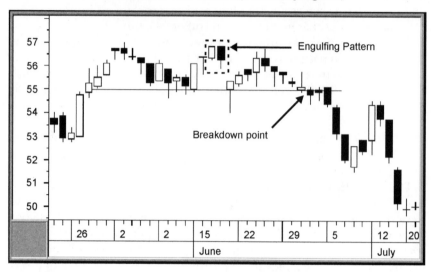

Chart 3-3 General Motors and three-river bottom. (Source: *pring.com*)

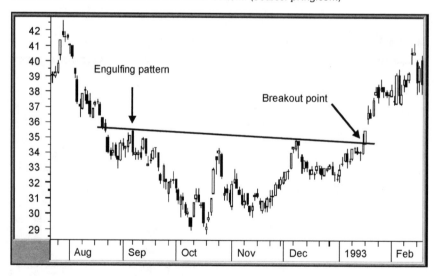

Tower Tops and Bottoms

Tower tops (Fig. 3-20) develop after a rally has been underway and a series of relatively long rising candles gives way to smaller ones, which gradually make lower highs. Finally, a long, black, down day indicates the rally is over. The signal develops when the gradualism of the steadily declining small real bodies gives way to the extreme movement, as depicted by the long, black real body. In this instance, the small real bodies indicate a balance between buyers and sellers that is slowly tipping to the sellers. The long black day puts this beyond reasonable doubt.

Tower bottoms (Fig. 3-21) form in the opposite way. A series of long, black, declining days are followed by a series of small candles where a new low may be grudgingly made, but after a couple of sessions, the candles gradually rise as higher lows are traced out. Finally, the price experiences a strong, long white day, and a reversal is signaled. It is important for the long white day to be accompanied by a good expansion of volume.

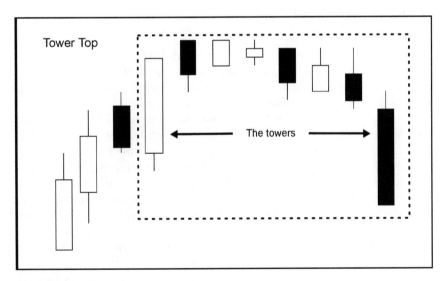

Figure 3-20   Tower top.

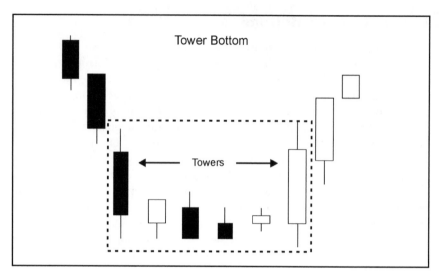

Figure 3-21 Tower bottom.

Dumpling Tops and Fry Pan Bottoms

The *dumpling top* is a form of subtle tower top (Fig. 3-22) in that the top-ping-out process is more of a slow gradual change in the balance between buyers and sellers. All the real bodies are usually quite small, and the market makes a form of rounding-top like a convex curve.

The dumpling corresponds to our own rounding top. The major difference is that the Japanese patterns should have a window or gap (Fig. 3-23), which indicates the urgency of the new price trend. In the case of a dumpling, the window would develop on the downside. This is the signal that the top has been completed and that lower prices are expected.

A *fry pan bottom*, alternately (Fig. 3-24), is the opposite of a dumpling top. It corresponds to the western rounding, or saucer, bottom and is formed with a concave type of price action, where the price falls sharply at first, then loses downside momentum, and gradually turns around. As with the dumpling top, the principal difference between the Japanese and Western versions is the appearance of a window (Fig. 3-25), as buyers become substantially more aggressive. Volume with a fry pan bottom and dumpling top

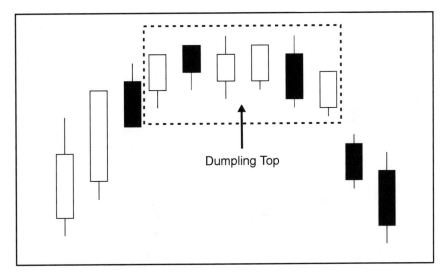

Figure 3-22   Dumpling top.

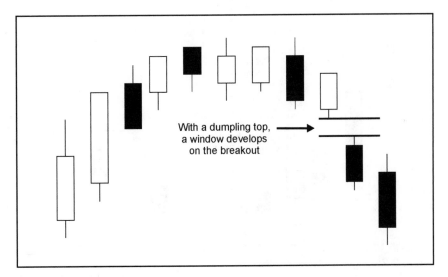

Figure 3-23   Dumpling top requirement.

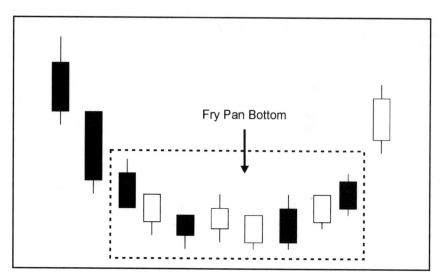

Figure 3-24 Fry pan bottom.

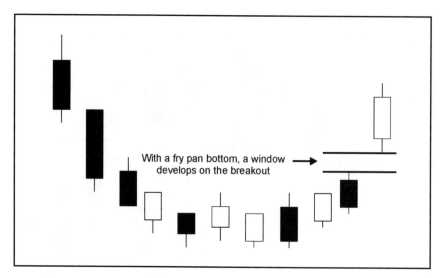

Figure 3-25 Fry pan bottom requirement.

should develop in a concave manner by shrinking in the middle of the pattern and gradually increasing, as the price drops in a dumpling or expands in a fry pan.

4

Marketplace Examples of Reversal Formations

Consider Chart 4-1. A tweezer bottom develops in June as flagged by the horizontal trendline. A small rally is terminated by a shooting star. Notice how the black candle following the "star" confirms by closing into the body of the long white candle that preceded it. While there was no way of knowing where the decline would end, it is worth noting that the low of the long white candle at point A was the real body low for the decline. This reminds us of the rule that tops and bottoms of long candles often act as important support and resistance areas. After the decline had run its course, a rally is signaled with a nice engulfing pattern around the 19th of June.

At the beginning of July, a good example of a bearish engulfing pattern develops. Note that the two high points of the real bodies, the close for the white body and the open for the dark one, are identical. This still counts as an engulfing pattern, provided the low for the black day engulfs the opening for the white one, which it does. Had both real bodies been identical in size, this would not have counted as an engulfing formation.

The decline did not last very long, which is not uncommon, because candlestick formations do not have a lasting effect on prices. A small rally ensues, then a dark cloud pattern forms. Remember the rules: after the market has been rallying, which it has, the first day should be a long, white real body. Then the second day should be a black real body, which opens higher than the first day and closes below the midpoint of the first.

Chart 4-1   General Motors and selected patterns. (Source: *pring.com*)

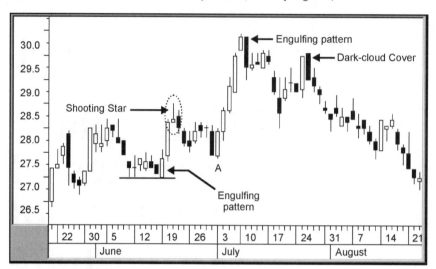

A series of engulfing patterns is shown in Chart 4-2. I have used it to demonstrate how candlestick patterns can have very short-term forecasting implications. The first one (point A) followed a small decline and another at point B indicated a decline of a similar duration. A four-day rally follows, and then another engulfing pattern (point C) forms. Since this rally was relatively brief, so was the new trend signaled by the pattern: one day, in fact. Then we see a dragonfly doji, a form of a bullish hammer, and the price bottoms. Finally, another engulfing pattern develops (point D), this time signaling a decline lasting barely a day. In a very general sense then, we can see from this and the previous chart that the power of a candlestick pattern often depends on the nature of the trend it follows. For example, a pattern that forms after a long uptrend, say, a couple of weeks, will have a tendency to be stronger than one that appears after a 2- or 3-day price move. I say "tendency" because there are no guarantees in technical analysis.

As the rally progresses you can see that a long white day (point E) is followed by two smaller black days. These are contained within the trading range of the first, so when the third white day closes at a new high, we have a form of rising three methods (see next chapter for a full description of this pattern); in this case, it is two contratrend days, so it is really a rising two methods.

Finally, we can see a dark cloud right at the peak of this rally. See how the second day opens above the first and then closes just a little bit below the midpoint of the white real body.

Chart 4-2 Coca-Cola and engulfing patterns. (Source: *pring.com*)

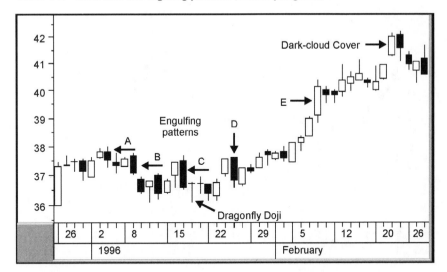

Chart 4-3 shows a Chicago futures chart for the yen. One thing you may notice is the substantial number of gaps or windows early on the chart. This is because a considerable amount of trading is done outside of the Chicago time zone. We see the same kind of phenomena in securities that are very illiquid. It is very important to bear this in mind when interpreting candlestick charts. What may appear to be a gap, may be just a distortion due to time zone differences or just plain illiquidity in the marketplace.

This chart shows a pattern that meets all the requirements of an upside-gap with two crows. It is preceded by an uptrend culminating in a long white day. The session sees an upward-gapping black day, followed by a second black day, which opens at around the same level as the first's real body and then closes below it. The close of this engulfing candle is still above the close of the long white day, that is, a gap is still present.

Chart 4-4 shows a shooting star, because the black upside-gapping day opens and closes close to the low, resulting in a small real body and a relatively long wick. Since the second black day still maintains the gap above the first day's opening, you may think that this could be an upside-gap with two crows. However, this pattern requires that the second black day engulf the first, which it clearly does not.

The bottom of the decline is signaled by a gravestone doji. This is normally a bearish pattern when it appears after an advance, but occasionally can be bullish after a decline.

Chart 4-3 Japanese yen and selected reversal patterns. (Source: *pring.com*)

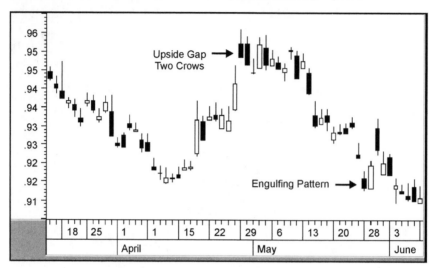

Chart 4-4 Kansas City wheat and selected reversal patterns. (Source: *pring.com*)

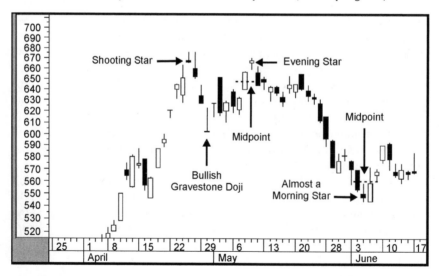

The next top is signaled by an evening star. The qualifications are a long white candle (that is, the color of the first day should be in the direction of the trend), followed by a small real body that gaps up from the first day (the color is not material in this case), and finally, the third day is a black candle that closes well below the midpoint of the first day (the midpoint, in this case, is indicated by the horizontal line).

The last formation highlighted on this chart is what I call an "almost-a-morning-star." This is because the pattern has most of the necessary attributes, except one. The first day is a long black body, which is in sympathy with the trend. The second is a small real body that gaps down. The third day is a long white candle, but it does not meet the requirement of a morning star by closing above the midpoint of the first day of the pattern. In this case, the halfway point is indicated by the horizontal line.

Chart 4-5 shows a very good example of a harami on September 22nd. During the early part of the month, the silver price experienced a protracted decline. Then, following the second long black day, a small candle is formed inside its real body. Remember, the upper and lower shadows of a harami do not have to be engulfed by the previous candle, only the real body. In this case, it does not matter because the whole candle is engulfed, and the decline is halted for quite a while. Note also the October 6th sell-off is halted by a small doji, which falls within the body of a black candle. This is a harami cross. It is not a very strong example because a good harami cross should be preceded by a sharp price movement and the preceding two-day decline does not really count. The whole bottoming process between approximately September 18th and October 7th is really a tower bottom. You can see how the bottom starts off in a frantic way with lots of selling, as indicated by the long black candle. Then supply and demand come into balance, as the price experiences a nice trading range with lots of spinning tops. Finally, the indecision is resolved on the upside, as the price breaks out with a strong white day. Normally, we would expect to see a stronger rally than this following the breakout from a tower bottom. However, the period covered by this chart represents part of a protracted 1-year downtrend in the silver price. Generally speaking, bullish candle patterns will have less effect in a bear market, and vice versa.

Finally, see how the top part of the long black candle serves as resistance for the next rally. The resistance level is not exact, but it can certainly be appreciated that tops and bottoms of particularly long candles often act as critical support and resistance areas for subsequent price action.

Chart 4-5   *Spot silver and selected patterns.* (Source: *pring.com*)

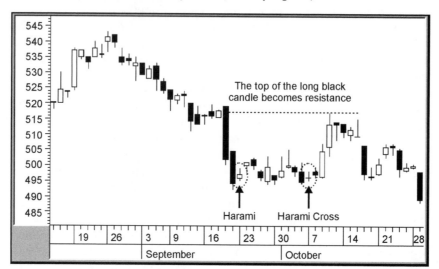

At the top of the rally in the left-hand part of Chart 4-6, two tweezer tops form at points A and B. A tweezer top is where two candlesticks have an identical high following an advance. The three black candles that form part of the second top have been labeled "three black crows" with a question mark. This is because they do not quite fit the strict definition of this formation. It is true that all three black candles appear at a high price, that is, after a rally. However, each crow should really close at, or near, the low of the day, and the first one does not really meet this requirement. Finally, each crow should technically open within the real body of its predecessor, and the third one definitely does not. Even so, there can be no mistaking the fact that this pattern was followed by a pretty nasty decline. The low point of this retreat was signaled by a harami. Normally, the first day of the harami develops in the same color as the prevailing trend. In this instance, a downward price movement would indicate a black candle, but here we see a white one. Similarly, the second day of the pattern is usually a different color than the first, though this is certainly not a prerequisite.

Also worth noting on the chart are two long-legged dojis at points C and D. Both signaled short-term declines. It is interesting to see how the real bodies on either side of these two patterns appeared below the two respective doji lines.

Chart 4-7, featuring Chrysler, was preceded by a decline and the first candle is a hammer. The lower wick is unusually long, given the trading

Chart 4-6 Ford Motor and selected reversal patterns. (Source: *pring.com*)

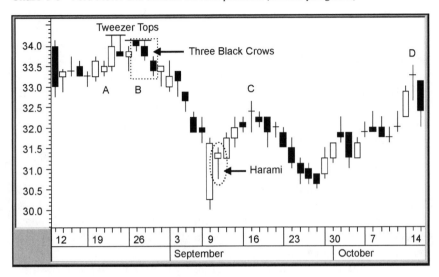

Chart 4-7 Chrysler and selected reversal patterns. (Source: *pring.com*)

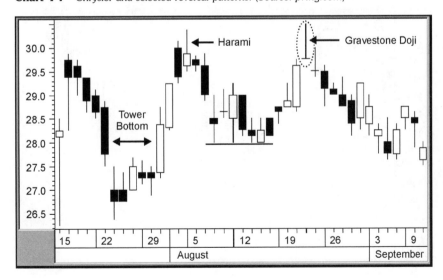

pattern of this stock. Also unusual is the fact that it is immediately followed by a hanging man. Normally, they would be separated by a rally lasting several days or even weeks. However, in this case, the upthrust in prices was so great that what would normally have taken quite some time was achieved in two days.

The ensuing decline was terminated by a tower bottom. The two arrows point out the two towers, first, the long black day, and then the bullish, long white day. Normally, the period between the towers is characterized by a sideways trading range, but in this case, the price started on its low and gradually worked its way higher until the second tower began in earnest.

The rally was ended with a harami. This pattern is not usually as reliable as the engulfing formation but, in this case, was followed by a three-day decline. The horizontal support trendline that formed in early to mid-August flags a multi-day tweezer bottom. What is interesting is the fact that the advance began with two black candles. Normally, we would have expected at least one of them to be white. The rally was halted somewhat dramatically by a gravestone doji.

Chart 4-8 features the March 1997 Treasury bond contract. It shows how important opening and closing prices can act as support and resistance areas. See how the horizontal line in January acts as resistance on about eight different occasions. Several times the price rallied above it on an intra-day

Chart 4-8 March 1997 T. bonds demonstration of support/resistance areas. (Source: pring.com)

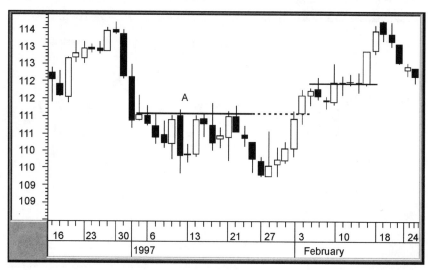

basis, but at no time did it open or close above the line. Also worth noting is the fact that the January consolidation (point A) lasted for twelve days. Seven of them were black and five were white. Quite often, a clue is given as to the direction of a breakout by the color of the majority of the candles. In this case, the majority was black and the price declined.

The horizontal level of resistance around 111 was still important during the ensuing rally, as indicated by the dashed line. It was eventually breached with a white candle that opened above it. The horizontal line in February also represented resistance for the opening and closing prices. Eventually, the price breaks out on the upside with a strong white line. Whenever a support or resistance level is breached by a long candle, the breakout is far less likely to be a whipsaw and is more often than not followed by a relatively powerful move. This is because supply and demand are fairly evenly matched during the consolidation phase prior to the breakout. In this example, the fine demand/supply balance is reflected on the chart by several dojis. If the breakout had developed with a small white line, the balance would have shifted to the bulls, but the long white line indicated a massive shift in short-term psychology, as if everyone wanted to get through the door at the same time.

Chart 4-9 features a tower top. The two arrows flag the two towers on the right and left. It is what happens between them that is perhaps of greatest

Chart 4-9   General Motors, 1994–1995, and a tower top. (Source: *pring.com*)

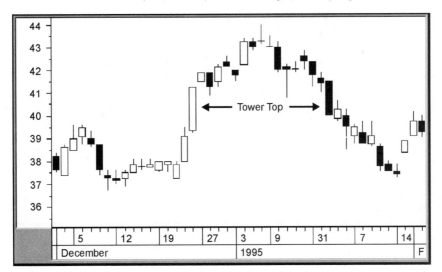

interest, since the rally was capped by a doji star. The first one, at the absolute peak, is almost a perfect gravestone doji. The second one certainly is. The whole pattern based on the real bodies gradually tips over from the top and starts to accelerate, as it approaches the second tower.

Also worthy of note is the December congestion area. It contains eight real bodies plus a doji. Since the breakout usually goes in the direction of the majority of the colors, it is not surprising that the 6-to-2 majority favoring the white candles was an upside one.

Chart 4-10 features a three buddha top, known in Western charting as a head-and-shoulders distribution formation. The second buddha (point B) is separated by two smaller ones (points A and C). They are smaller, that is, if measurement is confined to the height of the real bodies and not the shadows. The interesting thing about this pattern is that when the neckline is broken, the black candle on the day of the breakout is the third in a series of three black crows. Notice that each one closes at, or near, the low of the day and opens at, or within, the real body of its predecessor.

The sharp summer rally in Chart 4-11 ends rather abruptly with a counterattack line. I searched over many charts to find this one, as they are quite rare. You may recall that a counterattack line develops after an advance or

Chart 4-10   General Motors and a three-buddha top. (Source: *pring.com*)

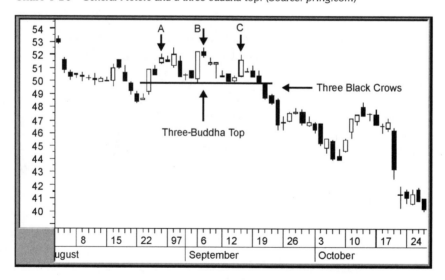

Chart 4-11   JP Morgan and a counterattack line. (Source: *pring.com*)

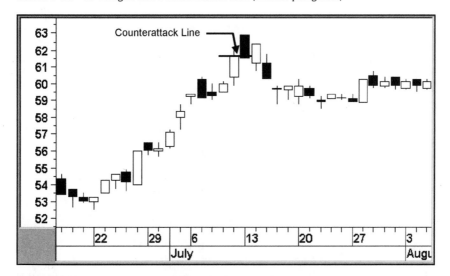

decline. In the case of an advance, look for a long white candle to be followed by a long black one, where the closings of both develop at approximately the same level. It really marks a kind of exhaustion move and was certainly followed by a spirited decline in this case.

Chart 4-12 features a couple more counterattack lines, alternatively known as *meeting lines*. The one at point A appears after a small rally, and that at point B after a decline. It is also worth noting that the real bodies for neither of these meeting lines were particularly large, so these are far from being classic examples.

The principal reason for featuring this particular time period in the JP Morgan price history is the inverted-three-buddha pattern, which is a special form of the three mountain bottom. The three arrows flag the three reactions, or three buddhas. Note the window (gap) separating the two real bodies on the breakout.

Finally, Chart 4-13 of Coca-Cola shows a dumpling top. It is not a perfect example, since a dumpling should consist of several small real bodies that form a sort of rounding top. This one has a couple of largish black candles on the right-hand side. Also, the two white candles on the left-hand side are a little longer than I would like to have seen. However, the overall feel of

Chart 4-12 JP Morgan, an inverted three-buddha bottom and counterattack lines. (Source: *pring.com*)

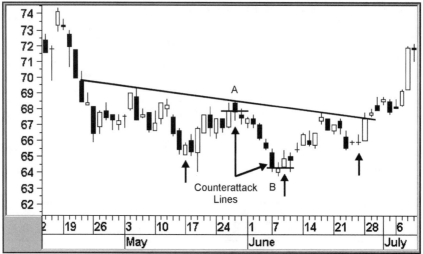

Chart 4-13 Coca-Cola and a dumpling top. (Source: *pring.com*)

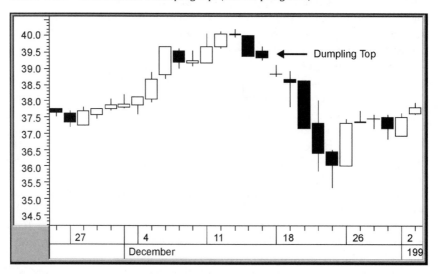

the pattern definitely has a rounding nature, which is a key ingredient of a dumpling top. Also, a downside window, or gap, is certainly present with the small doji star to the right. As you can see, the price experienced a nasty decline following the pattern's completion.

5
Continuation Patterns

The Concept

Continuation patterns occur within the confines of an uptrend or down-trend and represent only a couple-of-days-or-so consolidation. Following the completion of the pattern, prices are expected to resume the prevailing trend.

Rising and Falling Three Methods

Fig. 5-1(a) shows a bullish *rising three method*. This pattern consists of a long white candlestick forming in the direction of the prevailing trend. This is then followed by three or four declining small candles, ideally black in color. The important point is that the trading range for this series of declining lines remains within the high and low of the first strong white day, that is, within the two horizontal lines in Fig. 5-1(a). The pattern is completed with another strong white day in which the price opens at, or preferably above, the previous close and closes at a new high (Fig. 5-1b), that is, above the close of the first white candle. It is important for volume to contract on the black days and expand noticeably on the final white day. Strictly speaking, all of the small real bodies should fall within the trading range of the first long white candle. The key characteristic is that the two white candles represent a form of controlled profit-taking in an ongoing trend.

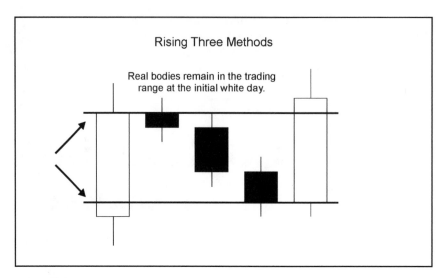

Figure 5-1a Rising three methods.

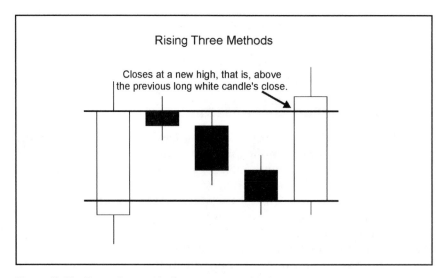

Figure 5-1b Rising three methods representing a breakout.

Consequently, if one of the interim candles falls a bit out of that range but still forms part of a controlled profit-taking environment, this should not unduly affect the positive nature of the pattern. The appearance of a third long white candle after the formation has been completed (Fig. 5-2) indicates that buyers once again have the upper hand, and an extension to the rally should then be expected.

The *falling three methods* (Fig. 5-3) occurs during downtrends. It consists of a strong black day followed by three or four small rising days, ideally white in color. As with the rising three methods, it is also possible to have as little as two small candles. The final day should open under the previous day's close and close at a new low for the move. Once again, the small candles that form between the two long ones represent a temporary digestion of losses where the battle between buyers and sellers is at a temporary stand-off. Consequently, if the final long black day, or the one following it as confirmation, is accompanied by heavy volume (Fig. 5-4), the validity of the pattern is increased.

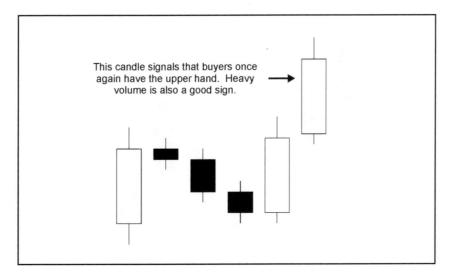

Figure 5-2 Rising three methods representing the confirmation.

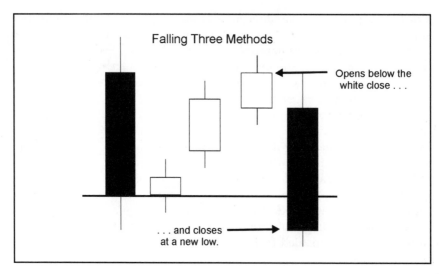

Figure 5-3   Falling three methods requirements.

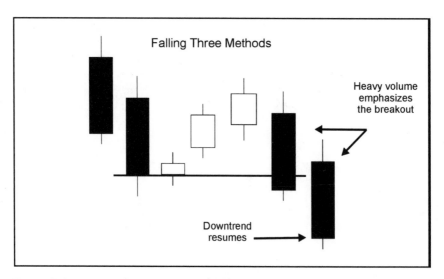

Figure 5-4   Falling three methods and confirmation.

Three Advancing White Soldiers

This pattern consists of three white candlesticks closing at progressively higher levels (Fig. 5-5a). The concept of the three soldiers is that they march steadily higher rather than running too fast. When this pattern appears after a consolidation, it portends higher prices to come. Ideally, the "soldiers" should experience a slow steady rise, where each white candle opens within the body of its predecessor (Fig. 5-5b). Also, each should close at, or near, its high (Fig. 5-5c). This means the soldiers should not experience much in the way of upper shadows. Long candles are generally bullish, but in the case of the advancing three soldiers, it is better for the white real bodies not to be overly long, otherwise the feeling of an overbought market creeps in and, since this is a continuation pattern, an overbought condition would be inconsistent.

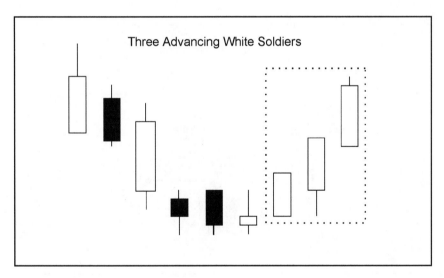

Figure 5-5a   Three advancing white soldiers.

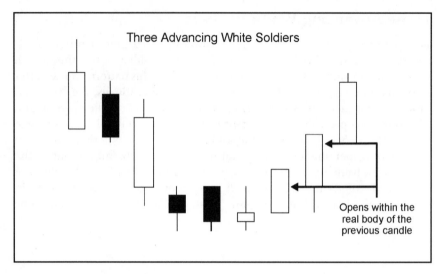

Figure 5-5b   Three advancing white soldiers requirements.

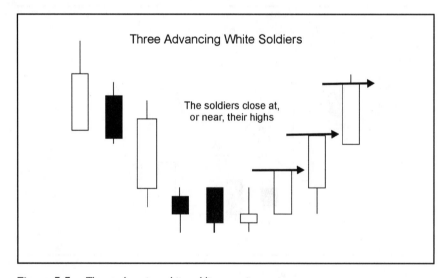

Figure 5-5c   Three advancing white soldiers requirements.

Alternately, if the second and third soldiers fail to make much net upside-headway (Fig. 5-6), this is regarded as a cautionary sign, and the pattern is then known as an *advance block pattern*. Be particularly aware of an advance block after prices have been rallying for a while and when the uptrend is fairly mature.

If the first two candles in the formation are long white days and the third contains a small white real body (Fig. 5-7), this is known as a *stalled pattern*. Both the stalled and advanced block patterns indicate a dissipation of upside momentum. They are not strong enough to be regarded as reversal phenomena, but they do hold out the possibility that a short-term decline or consolidation may get underway. Traders are then advised to take partial profits at least, though the signal is not normally strong enough to warrant a short sale.

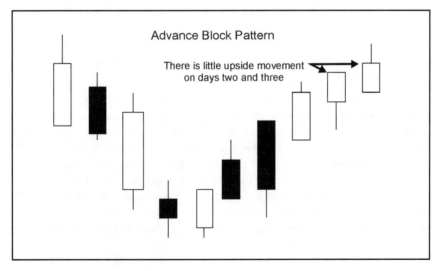

Figure 5-6   Advancing block pattern.

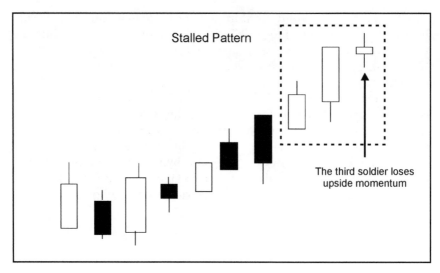

Figure 5-7   Stalled pattern.

Separating Lines

A *separating line* (Fig. 5-8) occurs when candlesticks of differing colors open at the same level. In an up market, the first day in the pattern is a long black candle, where the close is below the open. The next day is a long white candle, where the price opens at the same level as the previous day's open. In effect, the price on the second day opens higher than the previous day's close by an amount determined by the length of the previous day's real body.

In a down market, the process will be reversed, as the first day is a white candle and the second a long black candle opening at the same level as the first candle's opening price. In Fig. 5-9, we see two examples of separating lines in the same downtrend.

In the case of both the up- and downtrends expect the prevailing trend to continue, since these are continuation patterns.

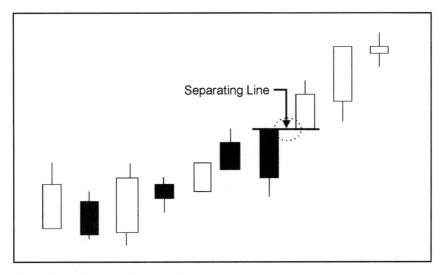

Figure 5-8   Separating line in a rally.

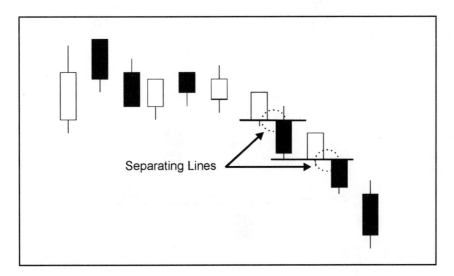

Figure 5-9   Separating lines in a decline.

Windows

In Japanese candlestick charting, a window amounts to the same thing as a gap in Western charting. A window develops when one day's price range is completely outside that of its predecessor. In Fig. 5-10, the window is indicated by the space between the two horizontal trendlines. It is normal for a window to be closed soon after it has developed in the charts. It is said that markets abhor a vacuum; well, in candlestick terminology, I am sure that markets dislike open windows because they are draughty. Therefore, every effort is made to close, or to at least attempt to close, an open window. Quite often, you will find the window that develops during an uptrend will offer support for a corrective price decline. That is exactly what we can see in Fig. 5-10, as two days after the gap, the opening price of the white candle finds support in the area of the lower horizontal line. Similarly, a window that occurs during a decline (Fig. 5-11) acts as resistance to a price rally retracement.

Windows that develop during a congestion area, when unconfirmed by a second candle, can be quite important. In Fig. 5-12 we see a window in a congestion area flagged by the two horizontal lines. The subsequent day opened at the high and closed the window. This was a long black candle, so the bearish closing price confirmed the negative trend originally in place before the appearance of the window.

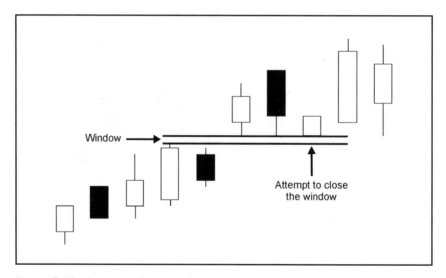

Figure 5-10 Attempt to close a window.

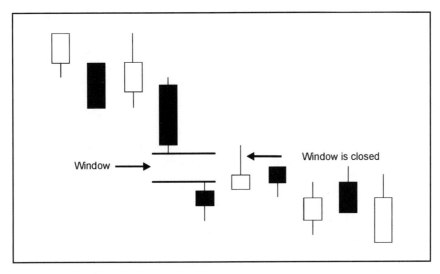

Figure 5-11   Window being closed.

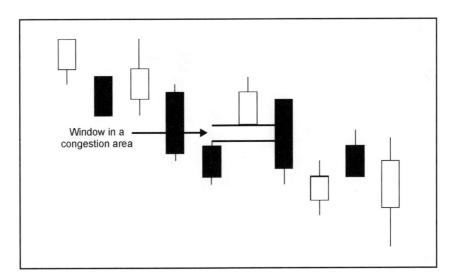

Figure 5-12   Window in congestion area.

When analyzing the various forms of windows, it is important to bear in mind the nature of the chart being monitored. For example, if you look at a U.S.-based futures chart of the Nikkei, a substantial number of gaps will be present because the majority of the trading is done in Tokyo in different trading hours. Consequently, the gaps have little meaning compared with those that develop on a Chicago bond chart, where the majority of U.S. bond trading is carried out. For this reason, it is always a good idea to study the chart of a security to make sure it does not fall into one of these illiquid trading sessions. The same comment concerning such irrelevant gaps could be made of very thinly traded stocks compared to highly liquid ones.

Upside and Downside Gaps

The *upside-gap tasuki* shown in Fig. 5-13 is formed during an advance when a white candlestick gaps up from another white candlestick. This is followed by a black candlestick, which opens within the previous day's real body and closes below the previous day's open. However, to qualify as an upside gap, the black candlestick must leave the gap created by the second day intact (Fig. 5-14). The upside gap is an emotional affair, where buyers enthusias-

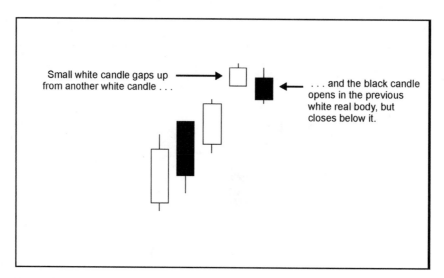

Figure 5-13 Upside-gap tasuki.

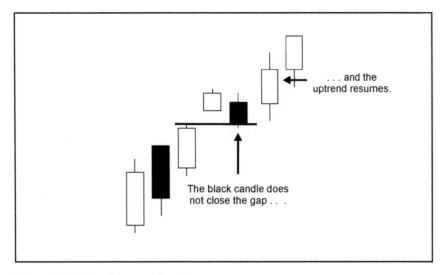

... and the
uptrend resumes.

The black candle does
not close the gap . . .

Figure 5-14   Upside gap confirmed.

tically bid up. The black day that follows is a test of buyer resolve, in that the price is able to hold above the closing level of the first white day. The buy signal, therefore, comes when it is apparent the price is not going to completely close the gap or *window,* as it is called in candlestick terminology. When the test succeeds with the closing price on the black candle holding above the close on the long white candle, the buyers are once again free to bid up prices. Alternately, if the black candle does close the gap and the real body falls well into the real body of the first white day, the bullish implications from the upside gap consolidation are cancelled.

The *downside gap* is the exact opposite. In Fig. 5-15, we see a black candlestick followed by a second black one, which gaps to the downside. Then a white candlestick opens within the black body of the second. It closes above the opening of the second candlestick, but does not close the gap. The failure to close the gap in this case (Fig. 5-16) indicates the bears remain in control and the downward trend should be expected to extend.

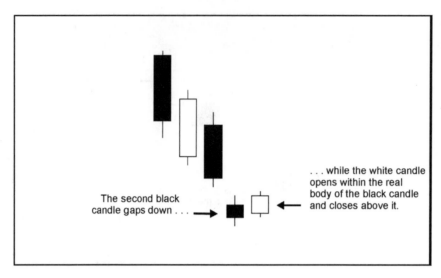

Figure 5-15 Downside gap.

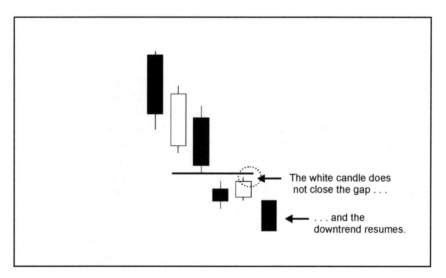

Figure 5-16 Downside gap confirmed.

High-Price and Low-Price Gapping Plays

The *high-price gapping play* (Fig. 5-17) is a gap that develops after prices have experienced a consolidation of previous gains. It gets its name from the fact it is often preceded by the several small real bodies that congregate around the previous price high. The small real bodies represent a form of controlled profit-taking in which the forces of demand and supply are fairly evenly matched. When the price gaps up, the battle has clearly moved in favor of the bulls.

The *low-price gapping play* is the exact opposite and develops during a downtrend (Fig. 5-18). After several days in which prices, as reflected in small real bodies, digest their losses, the price suddenly gaps to the downside, as a downside window is opened. This is a great example of why one should assume the prevailing trend is intact until the weight of the evidence shows or proves it has been reversed. This is because the consolidation, or digestion of losses, gives the appearance of a base or accumulation pattern to the optimistic bulls. However, this is a consolidation pattern, and anyone who would have anticipated otherwise would have experienced a nasty shock

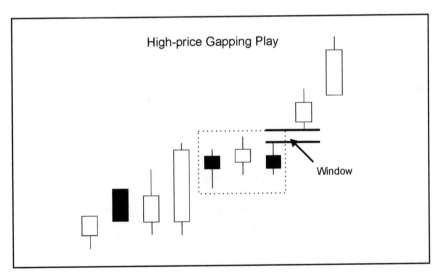

Figure 5-17   High-price gapping play.

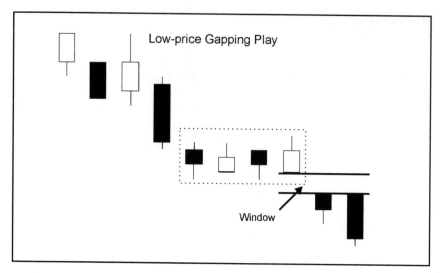

Figure 5-18   Low-price gapping play.

on the day the downside window was formed. In such cases, the only evidence a reversal had transpired would have been limited to the trader's head and not the tape!

Gapping Side-by-Side White Lines

This pattern consists of two small white real bodies that develop during an uptrend. The first one gaps above the previous session's trading range, and the second one opens and closes at approximately the same level as the first (Fig. 5-19). When the next day closes higher, a confirmation is given and prices are then expected to resume their uptrend.

The equivalent in a down market is quite rare because it is the norm in a declining trend for windows to be opened by black candles, not white ones.

Matt-Hold

The *matt-hold* that is illustrated in Fig. 5-20 is similar to the upside gap with two crows; however, unlike that formation, this one is a continuation pattern. It consists of the long white candle and two crows described earlier.

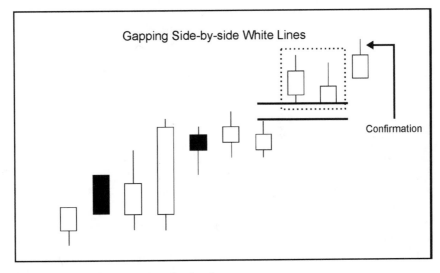

Figure 5-19   Gapping side-by-side white lines.

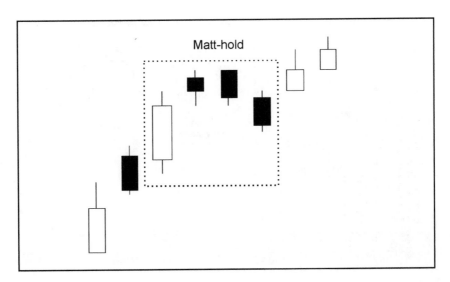

Figure 5-20   Matt-hold.

In addition, it includes a third black candle followed by a white one. To qualify as a matt-hold, this white candle must either gap above the upper shadow of the third crow, so to speak, or close above its high. Do not go looking for these patterns in every chart, because you will be disappointed, as they are quite rare.

Marketplace Examples

Chart 5-1 of JP Morgan features several gaps or windows. The one in early August is really a breakout from a fry pan bottom. In this instance, it is not really a bottom, since there has been no decline, only a consolidation. In any event, the characteristics of a fry pan are all there. The concave price action is followed by a window, and later the window was closed with an umbrella candle.

Trendlines are often violated in the middle of a window. This generally gives a far stronger signal than if it develops during a session when a small real body is being formed. In this chart, we see two very strong trendline penetrations, in late August and mid-September. Both violations occur as a window is being "opened."

Chart 5-1 JP Morgan and windows. (Source: *pring.com*)

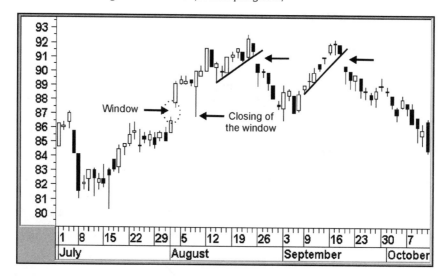

Merrill Lynch is featured in Chart 5-2, where three different continuation phenomena develop. The first, in early November, is a three-advancing-white-soldiers pattern. It offers a gradual, but steady, advance in which each soldier opens the session at, or within, the real body of the previous white candle. Each soldier closes at, or very close to, its high for the session. In January 1997 we see a variation of this formation called a *stalled pattern*. See how the length of the third day is considerably less than the second one. This indicates a dissipation of upside momentum and often signals a short-term temporary consolidation. Finally, we see a high-price gapping day in February. This pattern, you will recall, consists of a window candle that breaks above a small consolidation pattern. In this particular instance, the gap or window and the following long white candle are fairly dramatic.

A separating line is shown in Chart 5-3. This consists of two candles of differing colors. In a downtrend, the first candle should be white and the second, black. Both should open at the same level. In this respect, they are the exact opposite of the counterattack line, where the two closes are more or less identical. The separating line is a consolidation pattern and the attack line a reversal pattern. This is not a perfect separating line because the second day should be closer to a belt-hold, that is, with much smaller shadows.

Chart 5-2   Merrill Lynch and selected continuation patterns. (Source: *pring.com*)

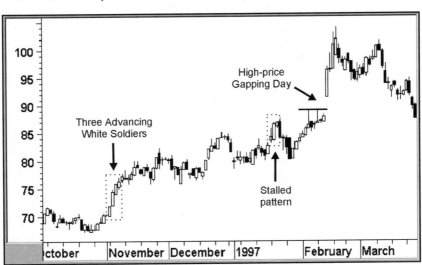

Chart 5-3 McDonald's and selected continuation patterns. (Source: *pring.com*)

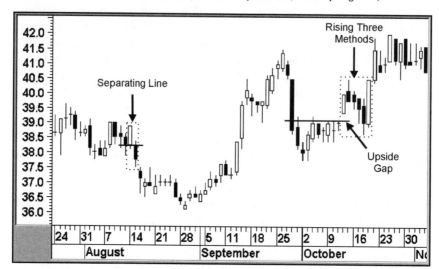

In October, an upside gap follows a consolidation formation. In this instance, the gap was closed fairy quickly but in an interesting way. This is because this pattern is a consolidation rising three methods. Strictly speaking, the real bodies of the black candles should fall within that of the initial white candle, and these do not. Nevertheless this formation definitely has the flavor of a rising three methods. Actually, there are four declining candles that more or less fall within the two strong white candles on either side. The resistance line shows how the extremities of unusually long candles often serve as important pivotal points for future price movements.

6

Blended Candles

A *blended candle* is a term invented by Steve Nison for a technique used to determine whether a candle pattern containing more than one candle line is bullish or bearish. It is described in detail in his excellent book *Beyond Candlesticks.* This Japanese technique arose because it is not always possible to understand the true implication of a candle pattern. The blended candle, therefore, helps point us in the right direction. The idea, as in Fig. 6-1, is to make a candle using the high and low of the two days as the upper and lower shadow extremes. Then, take the opening of the first day and the closing of the second. In this way, the blended candle is the same as if the two daily sessions were really one.

In this example, the two candles on the left are the individual days and that on the right is the blending of the two. See how the opening price of the first day becomes the opening for the real body on the right. The closing on the second day becomes that of the closing price. Then the extreme high achieved on the first day becomes the high for the blended candle, and the low for the two days, set on Day 2, is the bottom of the lower shadow.

The result is a candle that is bullish, because the real body of the white candle develops near the top of the trading range. In this case, the two-candle pattern on the left was a bullish engulfing pattern, which was relatively easy to identify. Other two-day patterns, though, are less obvious.

For example, Fig. 6-2 features one where a white real body is followed by a dark real body. The resulting blended candle turns out to be a shooting star. The opening occurs at the same level as the first day's opening and the closing the same as the second real body's close. Then the highest of the two highs is the second day and the lowest is the same as the first day's opening, since there is no lower wick. Shooting stars tend to be bearish candles after a rally and bullish after a decline. Note also the thick horizontal line on the first day. This is the halfway point of the real body. Had the price

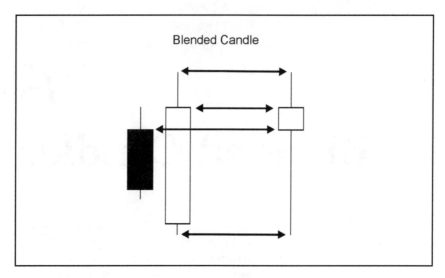

Figure 6-1   Blended engulfing pattern.

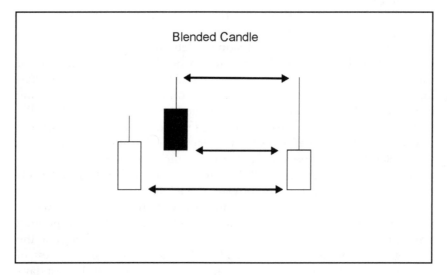

Figure 6-2   Blended stars.

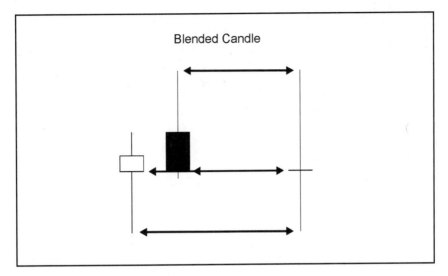

Figure 6-3 Blended shooting star.

closed below this level, the two-day pattern would have been classed as dark cloud cover, a bearish pattern.

Fig. 6-3 shows a final example, where opening the price of the first day and the closing price of the second are identical and result in a doji. Because of the large trading range, the blended candle formed a long-legged doji. The battle between buyers and sellers is pretty evenly matched in this instance.

II

Integrating Candles with Other Techniques

7

Candlesticks and Western Charting

Comparing Techniques

All charts reflect changes in the psychological attitude between buyers and sellers, which is what determines price trends. My definition of technical analysis is, *The art of identifying a trend reversal at a relatively early stage and riding on that trend until the weight of the evidence shows or proves that the trend has reversed.* In this context, it is the *weight* of the evidence that is important because candles are just one piece of evidence. It, therefore, makes sense to combine candle charts with other techniques to gain a wider understanding of what the evidence is really saying.

If we were looking at a Western chart, for instance, we would not only consider a price pattern, such as reverse head and shoulders, but we would also take a look at the volume configuration to see whether it expanded on the breakout. A prudent approach would also involve a quick look at several momentum indicators to make sure they were consistent, as well. In this chapter, we will see how candle charting can be included in this weight-of-the-evidence approach, concentrating on those offering the most promise.

Support and Resistance

Support and resistance are basic building blocks of Western technical analysis, and their use can greatly enhance the interpretation of Japanese candlesticks. Chart 7-1, for example, shows that the lower June/July line marks an important resistance area. It is a principle of the support/resistance concept that a specific support or resistance area gains significance from the number of times that it has been able to turn back a rally or reaction. Looking at the line and remembering that the top of a white real body represents the closing price for the session, it is possible to appreciate that on a Western close-only or line chart, this line would have been touched twice. However, since the candle charts place strong emphasis on opening prices, this line has actually been responsible for more reversals, since all the black candles should also be included. Using this method, the line has been touched an additional three times. Little wonder that when it was finally breached, the price experienced a worthwhile rally. Note that the lower shadow of the candle (point A) that developed just before the price fell below the line also found support there. Given the rule that a resistance level, once penetrated, reverses its role to support, this formidable resistance line should have acted as a barrier to further price erosion, once breached. And this, indeed, was the case, as the lower shadow of candle B terminated just a little bit above the line.

The second line offers a further example of this principle. In this instance, there were six white real bodies that found resistance at the line in a similar way to a Western closing chart. However, the candle chart experienced some additional reversals, this time from the opening prices, as reflected by some black real bodies. Notice also that the line reversed its role to

Chart 7-1   American Brands and resistance lines. (Source: *pring.com*)

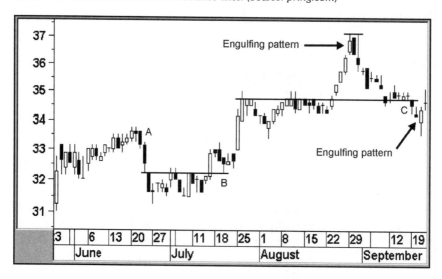

support on the return move, as it cuts straight through two black candles: a white one and a doji in the middle (point C).

Other points of interest in this chart include the bearish engulfing day at the top of the rally and the bullish engulfing day at the bottom. Also, the line touching the two upper shadows, right at the top of the August rally, indicates a tweezer top. At one time during the black day with the long upper shadow, it looked as if the engulfing pattern was going to fail. However, by the end of the day, the price had found resistance at the line and actually closed below the second day of the engulfing pattern. The pattern itself was bearish, but the failure of the price to cancel it, and the presence of the long upper shadow indicated beyond reasonable doubt that the uptrend was exhausted.

In Chart 7-2, featuring American Heritage, the December rally ends with a pretty dramatic shooting star. The upper wick is extremely large, but the main point of the chart comes from the fact that the lower part of the shooting star's real body subsequently turns out to be a very important short-term level of resistance. This is evidenced by the real bodies of four subsequent candles that fail to move above it. Finally, an engulfing candle develops at point A, and the reversal is signaled beyond reasonable doubt. In this instance, the second day is not an engulfing day in which the opening is above the previous day's real body, since this candle opens at exactly the same point as the high of the previous real body and then engulfs it on the downside.

Chart 7-2 American Heritage and a resistance trendline. (Source: *pring.com*)

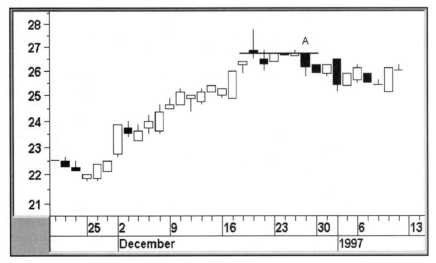

Here then is an example of a Western resistance technique that indicates there was a barrier to upside movement and Japanese candle methods, the engulfing pattern, that tell us that the trend is now down.

This leads us to another possibility. Suppose a price has rallied back to a previous high, as at point A in Chart 7-3. Using traditional Western techniques, a previous high is considered to be a point of potential resistance. How do we know whether this next rally will be able to surpass its predecessor? We do not, of course, but a review of the candlestick charts can sometimes provide a valuable clue. If, for example, a reversal pattern develops, then the odds of the previous high holding are pretty good. In this particular example, the attempt to break to new high ground failed. This was signaled by a bearish engulfing pattern, which was actually completed on the day of the high. A clear-cut signal of this nature could not have been given by a Western close-only chart. However, had this been a bar chart, the final day of the rally would have shown up as an outside day, since the whole price range completely encompassed that of the preceding day. (For an in-depth explanation of one- and two-day Western chart patterns, see *Technical Analysis Explained* by Martin J. Pring, 4th edition, McGraw-Hill, 2001.)

This concept of a resistance level being followed by an engulfing day appears to happen quite often. It is very useful, since the engulfing pattern confirms that the attempt on the resistance will end in failure.

Chart 7-3   Briggs and Stratton and support/resistance trendlines. (Source: *pring.com*)

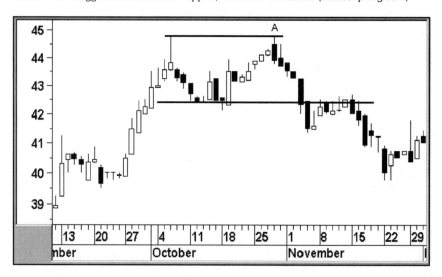

Trendlines

Candlestick interpretation can be usefully combined with trendline analysis. It is often difficult to know exactly where a trendline should be drawn with a candlestick chart. The question is, should the line join the shadows or the real bodies? The shadows mark the exact turning points, but since many of them occur on a fairly random basis, a proper reflection of the underlying trend is not always given. Alternately, joining the real bodies returns a line that connects more significant points but may not be touched or approached as many times. This is important because trendlines become more significant the larger the number of times they have been touched or approached. Since a trendline is supposed to reflect the underlying trend, it should be constructed in a way in which this objective is best accomplished. In effect, it is best to be flexible, using a little common sense, rather than relying on a hard-and-fast rule. Ideally, it would be better to draw lines that just touch real bodies, but if other trendlines make more sense, then they should be constructed, instead. The bottom line is that trendlines drawn on candlestick charts appear to work best when they join both shadows and real bodies. Occasionally, this will mean a temporary penetration, such as at points A1, A2, and B in Chart 7-4. However, if penetrations are acted on only when the line is violated by a real body, that is, an opening or closing price, fewer whipsaws will result.

Chart 7-4   Kellogg and a downtrendline. (Source: *pring.com*)

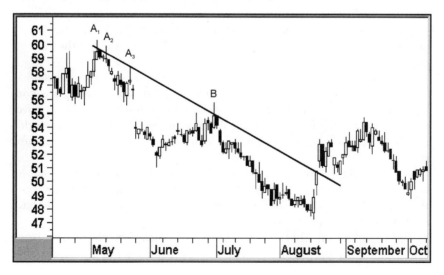

One of the great features of candles is that they often provide clues as to whether the price is likely to penetrate a line. Such clues are not always that apparent in bar-and-line charts. The downtrendline in Chart 7-4 actually began sometime before the initial plot and was therefore already established before the chart began. On an intraday basis, it looked as if a violation had materialized at A1. However, it soon became apparent that this was not going to occur because the black candle following the upper shadow breakout at A1 represented the second day of a dark-cloud pattern. You can see how the price opens higher, right at the line, but closes more than halfway down the real body of the previous white day. This dark-cloud formation indicated that the price was likely to experience a decline, which it did. At the end of that day, it should have been apparent to experienced candle chart watchers that the price was not going to rally above the trendline. The dark-cloud pattern only has a short-term significance, so it certainly did not offer any indication that the line would not be penetrated until August. However, it did imply that a violation would be delayed by at least three or four sessions at a minimum. Consequently, it would have paid to take a cautious stance during the formation of what turned out to be a long-legged doji at A2. As this candle was forming and the price broke out above the line, the action probably looked convincing. However, the very recent dark cloud cover would have suggested that it would have been wiser to temporarily overlook the breakout, until it could be seen how the session would close. Quite often, when a price violates a trendline during the session and is then unable to close through it, this indicates exhaustion. Exhaustion is usually followed by a sharp price move in the *opposite* direction to the false breakout. That was certainly true in this case.

Later on, at A3 a shooting star failed to penetrate the line. This pattern in itself indicates exhaustion, so again it was not surprising that the attempt on the trendline was quickly followed by a sharp decline.

In late June, at B the line once again proves to be overly strong resistance, as the opening price of the black day following the false intraday breakout turns out to be the high for that session. This is not a dark cloud cover because the two highs are at identical levels, but the negative feeling is definitely there and certainly confirmed when a window is opened on the next day.

Ironically, the day of the upside breakout in August is also a window and was preceded by two strong white days. The first long white day engulfs both the doji and the black day that preceded it. On a bar chart, this would have shown up as a strong outside day.

The trendline on Chart 7-5 has been constructed by connecting some lower wicks. The breakdown comes on a long black day. This is a negative

Chart 7-5 Schering Plough and an uptrendline. (Source: *pring.com*)

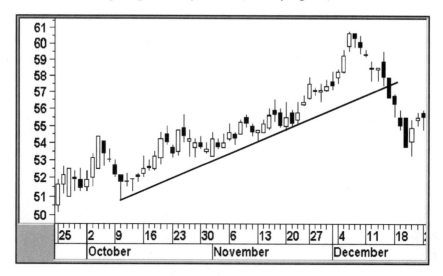

candle at the best of times, so the fact that it also occurs as a major support area (the trendline) is being breached makes it doubly negative.

This example also emphasizes an important point: *trendline breaks tend to be much more reliable when one or two other supportive technical characteristics are present.* For example, if the violation occurs on a day with a particularly long candle, this usually results in fewer whipsaws. Alternately, the penetration may take place, as the price literally goes right through a window. The idea is that both windows and long candle days represent strong swings in sentiment, which are more likely to result in a reliable signal. A small real body implies a relatively even balance between buyers and sellers, so a trendline penetration on such days is less likely to represent a reliable signal.

Other validations of trendline breaks might develop the day after an engulfing pattern, dark cloud cover, or piercing line, and so forth.

Price Patterns

Chart 7-6 of ABM Industries features a consolidation reverse-head-and-shoulders pattern. It is not that obvious from the candle chart, but when we place a Western close-only or line chart underneath, it becomes far more evident. One advantage of incorporating the candle chart into the analysis is that it can often give us a much clearer indication of the *manner* of the breakout.

Chart 7-6   ABM Industries and a line chart. (Source: *pring.com*)

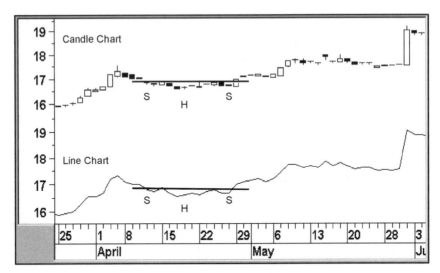

In this instance, the candle chart signals that the breakout day is an especially bullish one because it is the second day of an engulfing pattern.
Furthermore, it is also a relatively long white day, which adds even more support to the bullish case.

Chart 7-7 of AG Edwards shows a double bottom formation quickly followed by a head-and-shoulders or three-buddha top. What was the evidence,
if any, provided by the candle chart to suggest that the double bottom would
be completed with a successful upside breakout? Actually, there were two
clues. The first was a tower bottom at B2. Remember, a tower bottom consists of a long black day preceded by a decline. Then the market goes unduly
quiet for a few sessions. In this respect, you can see a doji toward the end
of the range and then a really small white real body. At this point, the sup-
ply/demand equation is pretty well in balance. Then, the final requirement
for a tower bottom, a long white real body, is met. The completion of this
pattern suggested that higher prices were in store, and this in turn implied
that a successful breakout above the rally peak at point C would take place.
The second clue came from the fact that the day of the breakout was the
third white day in which prices closed higher. In other words, we see a
set of three advancing white soldiers. When white soldiers appear after a
period of stable prices, then more strength is indicated. This is not a classic example, since the soldiers look as if they are more on a forced march
than a steady advance. The result is nevertheless the same . . . a good rally.

Chart 7-7 AG Edwards and two price patterns. (Source: *pring.com*)

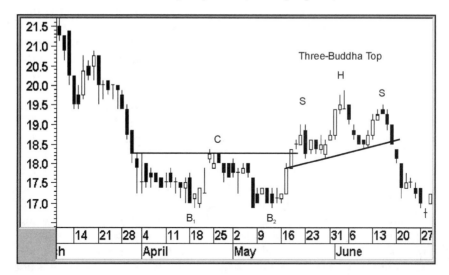

In bar or line charting, the measuring implication of the double bottom would be obtained by calculating the vertical distance from the low to the high point of the formation and projecting it up. Normally, this is a minimum objective because prices move much further though not necessarily in one move. In this instance, the measuring objective was the upper horizontal line at just under $20. Using candlestick methods, you can see that the objective was slightly exceeded on an intraday basis. However, the day of the high turned out to be a bearish gravestone doji. This suggested that the trend was at least temporarily exhausted. Thus, the (Japanese) gravestone doji and the (Western) price projection from the tower bottom could have been combined to more accurately predict a rally high of at least a short-term top.

As time progresses, the price traces out a head-and-shoulders pattern, or a three-buddha top. The right shoulder has the feeling of a tower top. A long white day is followed by a couple of small real bodies, indicating a narrowing balance between supply and demand. Then, there is the appearance of a long black candle on the day preceding the breakout. (This is the exact opposite of the day of the double bottom breakout, which opened on its low and closed on its high.) On the next day, the price breaks down and experiences a window as it opens on its high.

Originally, when the price broke out from the double bottom, it would have been reasonable to expect a larger rally than the one that actually materialized. However, once the three-buddha top had been completed, it should have been obvious, even to the most diehard of bulls, that the bullish implications of the double bottom had been more than cancelled out by the three-buddha top. The prudent thing to do at that point would have been to close out any open positions. After all, if you buy because of an anticipated event and that event does not take place, there then exists no reason to continue with the trade.

Chart 7-8 of Norfolk and Southern shows a support/resistance line that forms the top of a reverse head-and-shoulders and the bottom of a head-and-shoulders distribution pattern. Prior to the upside breakout, every time the price rallies to the line, it did so with a black candle. The first one, at point A, is a dark cloud cover. The second one, at point B, fails to trade above the previous day's long, white real body. The third time (point C) we see a *rickshaw man,* typically a bearish pattern after a good advance. In this case, the rally was relatively small, but the rickshaw man succeeded in bringing about a short-term consolidation, after which the price again attempted to break above resistance. Finally, the day prior to the breakout experiences a very long, white real body. The breakout day creates a window, so it is not surprising to see a correction develop. Support for the correction is given by the trendline, which now reverses its former role from resistance to one of support. Finally, the long, white real body at point D engulfs the previous day's black real body. Once it was realized that the price was going to

Chart 7-8   Norfolk and Southern and two price patterns. (Source: *pring.com*)

close above the black real body, a strong reconfirmation of the breakout was given.

The first time that the price reacts back to the line again, the candles give an indication that the test would be successful, since the white real body at point E forms within the long black one preceding it. This is a harami pattern. Note that it is the real body relationship that is important, not that of the shadows. If the shadows were the defining point, this would not be a harami, because the lower shadow of this session was below that of the long black candle. The price then goes on to register the head of a head-and-shoulders or three-buddha top. Incidentally, the minimum upside objective of the September/December reverse head-and-shoulders had already been exceeded by that point. Then a decline to the horizontal trendline develops and, as expected, it found support at the line (point F) again. This time we see a hammer. The second penetration attempt also fails. Finally, the break comes on the day of a long black body. A half-hearted intraday attempt (point G) to rally back above the line also fails, as the price forms a bearish shooting star. A common characteristic of trendline price pattern violations is that the day of the breakout either experiences a window, such as the upside breakout in December, or a long line, such as the black one on the downside breakout that took place in late February.

Finally, the March price action (enlarged in Chart 7-9) contains a downward-sloping right-angled triangle. It is possible to join the lower part of the real bodies with a horizontal line and the upper wicks with a declining one.

Chart 7-9   Norfolk and Southern and a right-angled triangle. (Source: *pring.com*)

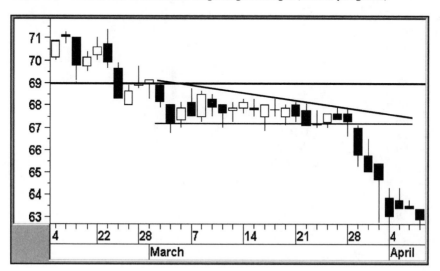

The lower shadows are either halted at the horizontal line or fleetingly penetrate it before closing at a higher level. Note that there is a predominance of black candles during the formation of this continuation pattern (ten black and seven white). Generally speaking, *the color that is in the clear majority during a trading range often gives a clue as to the direction of the breakout.* (Black majorities argue for a downside breakout, white ones for a rally.) In this case, the black dominance indicated the likelihood of a decline. On the day preceding the breakout, the small bearish engulfing pattern gave us more clues that the price was about to sell off. Finally, on the actual breakout day, the price opens below the line, tries to rally above it, finally experiencing a long black day.

Moving Averages

It is often a good idea to run a moving average through a candle chart and observe what the candles are saying, as the price comes close to, or penetrates, the average. Chart 7-10 features a 30-day moving average of Schlumberger. Note that with the exception of the long black day, when the price retreats back to the average in September, it is always the lower shadow that does the testing. This suggests that it is a half-hearted attempt, which it turns out to be. Whenever a wick threatens an average, the threat is never as great as when it is made with a real body. In this case, the two

Chart 7-10 Schlumberger and moving-average crossovers. (Source: *pring.com*)

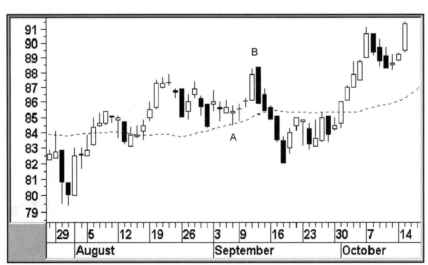

dojis at point A indicate that downside momentum has dissipated, and the price rallies. The next time it starts to decline, a more serious attempt at breaking the average takes place. First, a large engulfing pattern develops at point B. Engulfing formations only have short-term implications, but in this instance, the average is not far away and certainly within striking distance of the bearish effect of the engulfing formation. The actual penetration occurs on a black day, the third one in a row. As it turns out, the negative crossover is quickly reversed. This time it is the turn of a long white candle to undo the damage. Note that this candle actually experiences two buy signals, the moving-average crossover and the penetration of resistance marked by the top of the real bodies formed between September 16th and 29th.

Chart 7-11 features a 45-day moving average of the deutsche mark. The average is penetrated for the first time during a long black day, which makes it a fairly decisive violation. This candle happened to be the second in a series of three black crows. The break was also given credibility by the fact that earlier in the day, this candle had also penetrated the uptrend line.

The next time the average was penetrated on the upside, a window was opened. It is interesting to note that the retracement move that tried to close the window found support in the area of the average. Although the price did marginally penetrate it a couple of times, it was never able to experience a decisive violation with a real body. Then, when a real body crossover did materialize, it did so with a long black candle that opened a window in late November. This candle also succeeded in breaking below the small

Chart 7-11 Deutche mark trendline breaks and moving-average crossovers. (Source: pring.com)

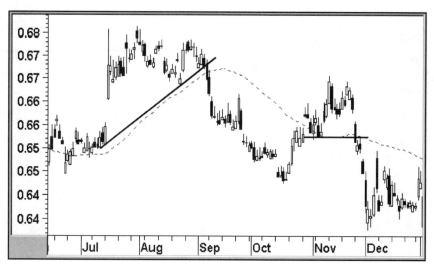

horizontal trendline. Whenever you see a reliable moving average and a good trendline in the same vicinity, they reinforce each other as support and resistance areas. Consequently, the joint penetration of these two support and resistance zones usually results in a more reliable signal.

Candles and Momentum

Combining candle patterns and momentum indicators can, at times, be more illuminating than comparing a momentum indicator with a line or bar chart. This is because the candles often show reversal patterns that are not so evident when using traditional Western charting techniques.

One very useful approach is to look for an overbought or oversold extreme in your favorite momentum indicator and then see whether there is any confirmation from the candlesticks. In Chart 7-12 we see an extreme oversold reading in the 10-day rate-of-change around January 12th. The oscillator itself is contained below a trendline, and later breaks above it. Almost at the same time, the ROC also completes a reverse head-and-shoulders pattern. This combination signaled beyond reasonable doubt that the downtrend in momentum had reversed, but what about the Nikkei itself? Well, the day that the actual intra-session low was made was a long white day that just missed being a perfect engulfing candle. This was followed by some dojis, which indicated that the balance between buyers and sellers was fairly

Chart 7-12 The Nikkei and a 10-day ROC. (Source: *pring.com*)

evenly matched. However, this had been the case in early and mid-December at points A and B. It was not until a few days after the momentum trend-break and inverse head-and-shoulders completion that a really positive sign developed, and that was this engulfing day at point C, just before the price broke above its December/January downtrendline.

Chart 7-13 of the British pound features a 14-day RSI. Quite often, it is a good idea to monitor the RSI to see when it rallies above its 70 overbought zone and then recrosses it on the way back toward equilibrium. I have marked an example with an arrow. Since the RSI often experiences divergences with the price, there is no guarantee that a decline will materialize a downward 70 crossover. For example, it could have gone on to make a new high and the RSI could have peaked below its October high. However, in this case, we see evidence of a reversal in the candles. The upward-pointing arrow under the price indicates a long black day following three small real bodies, the last one of which is a small shooting star. Also, it is possible to construct a resistance trendline joining all the real body highs that formed the peak of the rally. This would have made a great benchmark for a stop-loss for covering a short sale. The next day (following the arrow) is a long white candle that actually engulfs the previous day. At this point, it would have looked as if the rally was about to continue. However, this engulfing pattern was not confirmed, and the price was never able to experience an opening or closing above the resistance trendline. Remember, a pattern usually has to have something to reverse, and the engulfing formation

Chart 7-13 British pound and a 14-day RSI. (Source: *pring.com*)

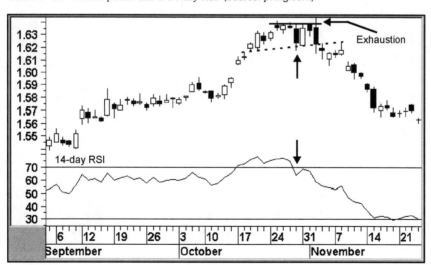

developed after a small consolidation and a strong rally. It was not, therefore, likely to be as strong as if it had developed after a decline. Eventually, the pound broke below the lower dashed trendline, thereby confirming the RSI sell signal. Note also that the intraday breakout above the upper horizontal trendline represented exhaustion. Little wonder that when the same candle broke below the lower dashed line, this was followed by a sharp decline.

Chart 7-14 shows the same approach, but from a reversal from a downtrend to an uptrend. The first time the RSI moved out of its oversold condition (A), there was nothing you could really point to from the aspect of calling a bottom. The next time (B), we see a piercing white line. The long white candle opens on its low and closes well into the upper part of the previous day's (black) real body. However, there is no real follow-through, and the piercing white line is only good enough for about 10-days of consolidation. The third time that the RSI bounces out of the oversold zone (C), it is associated with an engulfing pattern. See how the real body of the long white day totally engulfs the real body of the previous session. This tells us that a consolidation or small rally is likely. Since the downtrendline is not far away, the combination of the third RSI oversold crossover and the engulfing pattern warns us that the next session could well be the one in which the breakout materializes. And that is exactly what happened as a long white line successfully penetrated the 5-week downtrendline.

Chart 7-14   Canadian dollar and a 14-day RSI. (Source: *pring.com*)

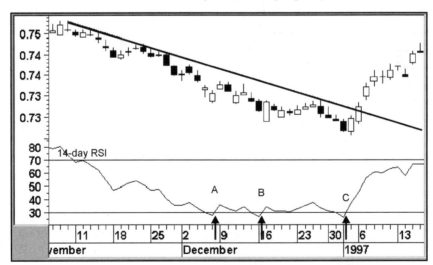

Since the RSI experiences a lot of occasions when it recrosses an extreme overbought or oversold zone, I prefer to smooth it with a moving average, as displayed in Chart 7-15. The series in question is an eight day moving average of a nine day RSI. The principles of interpretation, though, are the same. Look for an overbought or oversold crossover and then see what the candles are doing. In this particular example, the RSI sell signal is flagged by the downward-pointing arrow. The candles experience a window, as a spinning top precedes a small black candle. Since the window also occurred at the same time that the price was breaking below an uptrendline joining several real bodies, this emphasized the strength of the trendbreak.

One other point worthy of note is this bearish engulfing pattern at point A that followed the sharp run-up in price. Normally, we would have expected a decline of some sort to follow, especially as the engulfing day itself was a very long black candle, the longest candle on the chart, in fact. However, this bearish pattern was followed by a bullish engulfing formation, and the palladium price subsequently rallied. Even so, there was no follow-through, and the price eventually declined. A key point, then, is that when a bearish pattern that fails to work is followed by a bullish formation that also does not operate as expected, this is a sign that the battle between buyers and sellers is fairly evenly matched. Whereas spinning tops and dojis, for

Chart 7-15   Palladium and a smoothed RSI. (Source: *pring.com*)

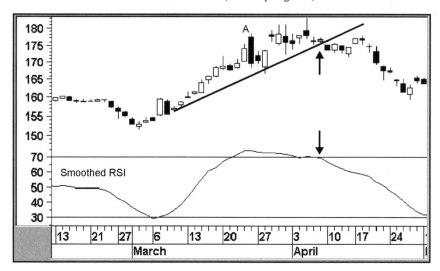

Chart 7-16   Palladium and a smoothed RSI. (Source: *pring.com*)

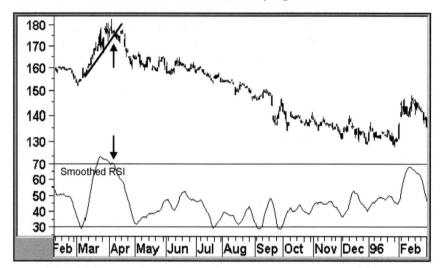

example, indicate a quiet balance, these contradictory engulfing patterns indicate a more emotional stand-off. Such high-pitched feelings are often the sign of an important turning point. Now if you refer to Chart 7-16, which puts Chart 7-15 into perspective, you can see that this emotional blow-off was followed by a long-term bearish price move.

III

Other Japanese Charting Techniques

8
Three-Line Break

Basics of the Three-Line Break

The *three-line break* is a form of candlestick charting that relies on a purely mechanical system using a filter (Chart 8-1). The basic concept is that once a trend gets underway, it is assumed to be in existence, until a countervailing signal is given. These reversal signals are predetermined and, therefore, are not subject to interpretation. The linebreak chart shows up as a series of black and white blocks that swing up and down. Actually, the correct terminology for these blocks is "lines." How are these trends determined? First of all, it is important to note that the three-line break method only deals with closing prices, so the candles on these charts do not contain upper or lower wicks.

Let us say that the market starts off in a bullish mode with a white line, as shown in Fig. 8-1. The next white line is drawn only when the closing high of this particular session is exceeded. This may take one session or several. If the closing high is not exceeded, then nothing is drawn. This means it is possible to experience several sessions without any change to the chart. Three-line break charts do not, therefore, correspond to candle charts, where each line represents a specific date. *Time, then, is not important for three-line break charts.*

You can see this from the date scale at the bottom of Chart 8-1. See how the months are represented by different widths, unlike candle charts, where each date is represented by an identical space.

Chart 8-1   A three-line break chart. (Source: *pring.com*)

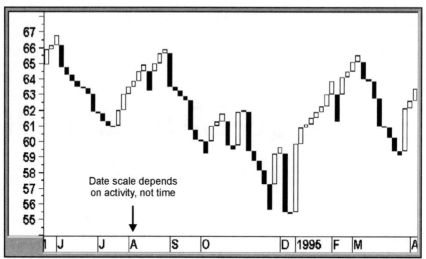

Figure 8-1   Three-line break, showing new highs.

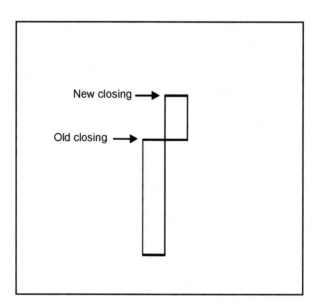

Reversals

A new series of black lines (Fig. 8-2) only begins when the closing price makes a new low for the move. In this case, it means the closing price must develop under the first white line. When a new closing low is established, the first black line can be plotted.

The principles for a reversal from a downtrend to an uptrend are similar (Fig. 8-3). In this case, look for a series of declining black lines. Then, when the closing price makes a high for the move, a series of white lines is begun, as in this example.

There is another, far more common, way in which a series of lines can be reversed. This occurs when there are at least three consecutive lines of the same color. In this case (Fig. 8-4), the low for the move is no longer below the first white line but is defined as a closing price which occurs below the previous three white lines. This is where the term *three-line break* comes in. Remember, every time a new closing high for the move is achieved, another white block is added, so the three-line break sell-signal is raised progressively higher. When the price closes below the third white line, a black line is plotted.

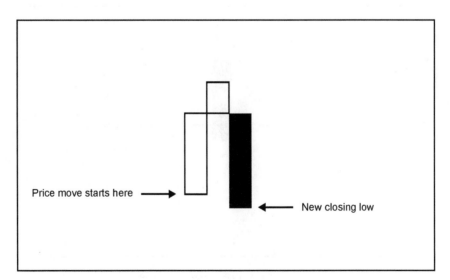

Figure 8-2 Three-line break, showing downside reversal.

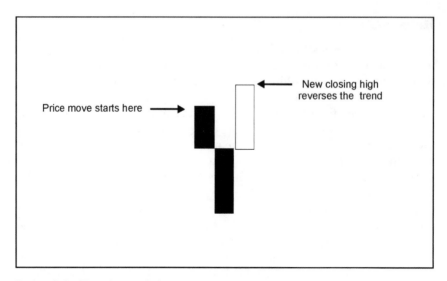

Figure 8-3   Three-line break showing upside reversal.

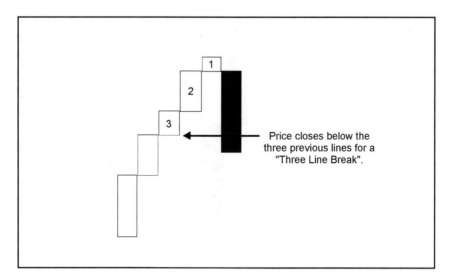

Figure 8-4   Three-line break, showing third-level downside break.

The same principle will apply in reverse, when a new uptrend is signaled after a series of black lines. As shown in Fig. 8-5, a series of new white lines will begin only when the closing price exceeds the closing price of the three previous black lines. Incidentally, the reversal line, that is, the line for which the color changes, is known as a *turnaround line*.

The vertical size of each black line will depend on the difference between the new low and the closing low; and for white lines, the difference between the old closing high and the new one. If the new low is a marginal one, such as that at arrow A in Fig. 8-6, the lines will be small. However, if a low is sharply lower than its predecessor, the line will be far longer. If the price fails to make a new low or does not close above the previous three black lines, absolutely nothing is drawn.

In summary, it is this series of three consecutive lines of the same color that gives its name to the three-line break. This technique is a filtering approach, which assumes that three consecutive higher closes reflects a strong trend. Consequently, this method requires a strong reversal signal to cancel the trend. In a situation where three consecutive days of the same color do *not* develop, the true direction of the trend is in doubt, so the rules for the reversal signals are less stringent.

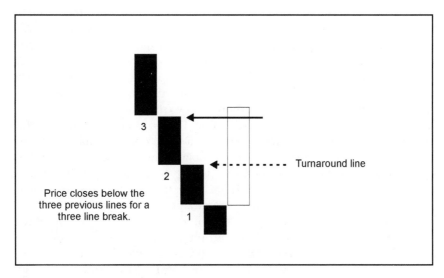

Figure 8-5 Three-line break, showing third-level upside break.

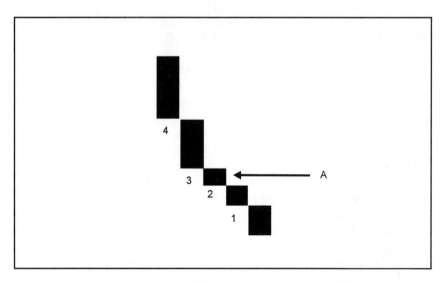

Figure 8-6   Three-line break, showing small price decrease from new low.

Chart 8-2 is a three-line break chart of JP Morgan. A new uptrend is established on April 8, due to the price closing above the black line at approximately $64. The triggering point is marked by the horizontal arrow (A). Since everything is based on closing prices, a reversal would not have been confirmed, until the top of the white line developed at a price a little above the $64 level. The April 8th plot was, therefore, the turnaround line. Once a new trend has been established, there are two things to monitor from the point of view of constructing the next line. First, a close above the April 8 closing, however small, will mean it will be a white one. Alternately, a close below the low of the move will generate a black line. In this case, the move began at arrow B, the low part of the white line. No more plots will be made until one of these levels is violated. In this case, the next line was quite small because the closing price was only marginally higher than the close just above arrow A. After that, the price continued to rally. However, this gives a false sense of security, since it looks as though there was no reaction whatsoever by the price. Chart 8-3, which features a candle chart for the same period, puts the record straight. April 8, the day of the three-line break buy-signal, is indicated by the arrow. As you can see, the timing was not so great, since the signal was given right at the top of the rally. The price then began to retreat, but *because it did not take out the low for the move set on April 4th at about $60, no black lines appeared on the three-line break chart.* This would have been quite an uncomfortable correction to sit through, since the price retraced most of the previous advance. Since it did not make a post–April 8th high or a post–April 4th low, nothing happens on the three-line break chart until mid-May, when the price closes at a new high (point A). Now, if you refer to the month of April, in Chart 8-2, you see the date scale was very narrow, meaning that there were very few plots. Compare this to the relatively large space taken up by June and July. As time progresses, six white lines develop. Then the price closes below the horizontal line at C (Chart 8-2, again), indicating that it is below the previous three white lines and a signal of a new downtrend is triggered.

Under the three-line break system, buy and sell signals are triggered when the line changes color, as indicated in Chart 8-2, that is, at the close of the turnaround day. As you can appreciate, this approach does not work very well in trendless markets, where the signals alternate between buy and sell with great regularity, and this is one of its drawbacks. However, once a series of three consecutive white or black lines develop, the odds of a trending market increase. The three-line break method then comes into its own. Another disadvantage is that a trend reversal is only signaled when the price closes below a series of three consecutive white lines or above a series of

Chart 8-2   JP Morgan and a three-line break. (Source: *pring.com*)

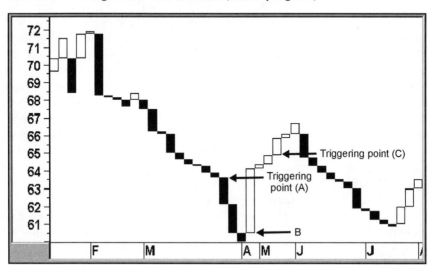

Chart 8-3   JP Morgan and a candlestick chart. (Source: *pring.com*)

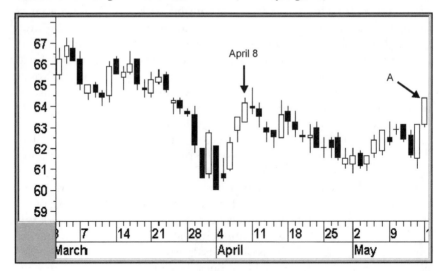

three consecutive black lines. This means that signals can occur well after
the turning point, as we saw in the JP Morgan example. However, since the
appearance of three lines of the same color usually results in a worthwhile
trend, it is an insurance premium well worth paying.

Bearing in mind that one should never trade or invest based on one indicator alone, it is often a good idea to combine candlestick or some other
analysis with the three-line break. For example, if a buy signal develops well
above the low, there is always the alternative of totally ignoring it. After all,
there is no reason why anyone *has* to buy, so why go out on a limb for a risky
trade? Having said that, there is one reason why a trader may need to make
a purchase and that is to cover a short position. In such a situation, it is better to cover the short when, during the session, the price moves decisively
above the closing level required to trigger a turnaround day. This then offers
protection if the price does, in fact, close much higher. Alternately, if the
session does not materialize as a turnaround day, the short position can
always be reinstated, provided the price does not close substantially below
the three-line break triggering point.

Let us say we are considering making an outright purchase on April 8th
(Chart 8-4), the turnaround day. In that case, it would be a good idea to
review some other indicators; or, since the price had already advanced quite
a bit, wait for a reaction. If you recall, the top of the white day (point A)

Chart 8-4 JP Morgan and a three-line break. (Source: *pring.com*)

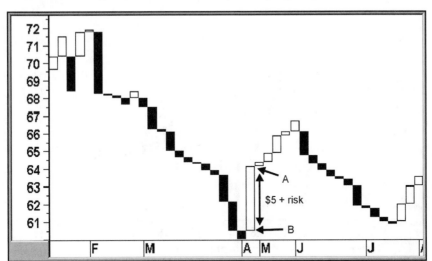

marks the point of entry, but under the three-line break rule, we would have had to risk just under $5, since the stop would be placed at around $60 (at point B). Of course, if the turnaround line closed well below $60, this would have represented an even greater risk, since the exit point is determined by the closing price, and it is not known until the actual close whether a reversal signal is triggered. This is why the notation on the chart indicates a risk of $5-plus. Alternately, had it been determined that the risk was too great and that it was more prudent to stake out the situation in the event of a reaction, our patience would have been rewarded. In fact, there were quite a few opportunities, as reflected in Chart 8-5.

For example, good support was represented by the horizontal line joining the bottom of the four real bodies. At first this would not have been obvious, but after the third or fourth attempt at violating the line had failed, it would have been obvious that the line was a minor support level. In any event, the three-line break approach would have justified making a purchase because it was still positive. The difference is, *this time the entry point would have been much lower.* Alternately, it was possible to construct a downtrendline and wait for an upside breakout (B). Finally, the long white candle on May 15th (C) engulfs the previous day's black candle for a classic short-term buy signal. This was higher than the other entry points but still lower than the original entry point at $64. A bullish engulfing pattern of this nature

Chart 8-5 JP Morgan and a three-line break RSI. (Source: *pring.com*)

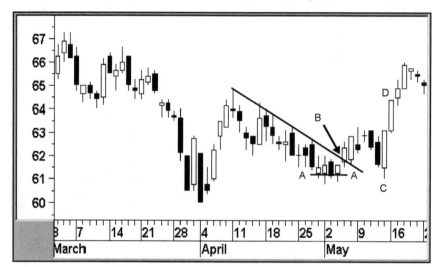

would have represented a much more reliable signal. The day after would have confirmed the trend beyond reasonable doubt, since it took out the previous rally high with a long white day (D).

In any branch of technical analysis, it is important to rely on more than one indicator before coming to a conclusion, and that is exactly what we have just done by combining candle and trendline analysis.

This concept is extended in Chart 8-6. The three-line method signaled a trend reversal signal on the 16th at point A, and it was a reasonably good indication, since the price declined for a while. Chart 8-7 shows a candlestick chart for the same period. In this instance, the price had been tracing out a three-buddha-top formation. The turnaround line for the day of the three-line break sell-signal just happened to be the day of the downside breakout (A). In this example, candles are being used to confirm three-line break signals. However, there is no reason why oscillators cannot also be included in the analysis. For example, if a bullish turnaround line develops when the 14-day RSI is very overbought, the odds would favor some kind of retracement. In such circumstances, it would be better to wait for the RSI to move back to a neutral, or even oversold, reading before making a purchase, and so forth.

Chart 8-6   JP Morgan and a three-line break. (Source: *pring.com*)

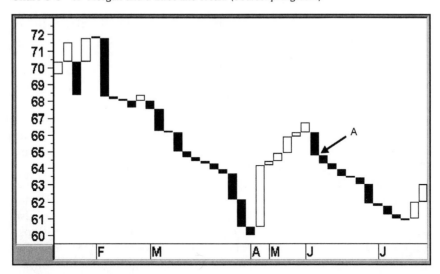

Chart 8-7   JP Morgan and a three-buddha top. (Source: *pring.com*)

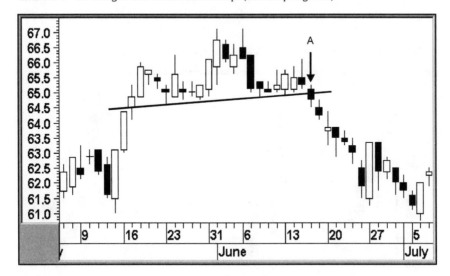

Three-Line Break Sets the Mood

In the JP Morgan example we used, the setback following the bullish three-line break signal on April 8th as an opportunity to search out a place to go long. It is possible to extend this idea by remembering the old adage, "A rising tide lifts all boats." What this means is that when you buy a rally in a bear market or short a reaction in a bull market, you are more likely to run into trouble.

One of the joys of the three-line break method is that it can be used as a signaling device to reflect the direction of the prevailing trend. Then the candles can be used to trigger buy and sell signals, but only those that are in sympathy with the trend and are signaled by the three-line break.

In Chart 8-8, featuring Merrill Lynch, a bullish three-line break is signaled on October 10 (1994) and runs all the way to November 14. Under our "rising tide lifts all boats" assumption, we should expect to see positive candle formations working and negative ones (contratrend formations) being less reliable. This bullish period is shown in the box in Chart 8-9. The first event takes place at point A, where a bearish engulfing pattern forms. It is true that the price experiences a minuscule decline, but the negative potential that we would normally expect from a relatively powerful formation, such as this, is just not present. Later on, at point B, another engulfing situation develops. This time the black candle engulfs several real

Chart 8-8   Merrill Lynch and a three-line break. (Source: *pring.com*)

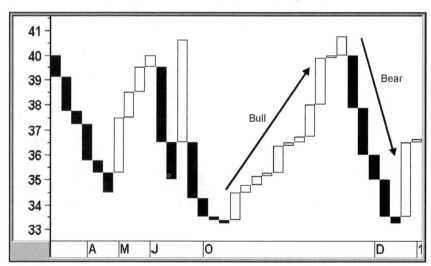

bodies, but instead of declining, the price rises. It is not a true engulfing pattern, of course, because the black day is preceded by a doji, not a long white candle. However, the fact that the black real body has a greater range than those preceding it for several days is normally a negative sign.

Alternately, the bullish formations do work, such as the bullish belt-hold and the sharp rally that follows it at point C.

Now, referring back to Chart 8-8, look at the next bearish three-line break-trend. It was signaled from November 21 to the buy signal on December 27. This same time period has been enclosed in a box on Chart 8-10. First, we see a contratrend bullish morning star (arrow A), which fails, whereas the pro-trend bearish engulfing pattern at arrow B succeeds. Also, at arrow C, we see a bearish doji evening star followed by a decline. A hammer literally hammers out a bottom right on the day of the low (arrow D). It is true that the bullish three-line break was not signaled until the 27th, almost two weeks later. Consequently, under the principles we are following, it would not have been prudent to have played the rally. However, the very fact the hammer worked would have been a valuable clue that the trend was probably in the process of reversing.

Please do not get the impression that every contratrend pattern or characteristic fails, and that every pattern that develops in the direction of the indicated three-line breaktrend works. This is definitely not the case.

Chart 8-9   Merrill Lynch and a candle chart. (Source: *pring.com*)

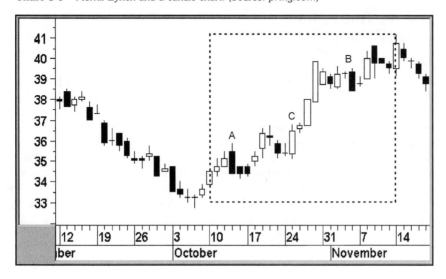

Chart 8-10 Merrill Lynch and a candle chart. (Source: *pring.com*)

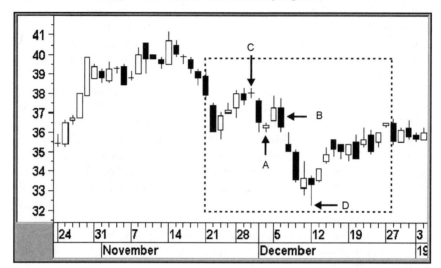

However, what we can say is, if a pattern or characteristic is going to fail, it is most likely to happen when it appears as a contratrend move, and vice versa. Consequently, by using the three-line break, you will be able to incorporate a very useful filter into your analysis.

Setting Three-Line Break Parameters

There is nothing magical to the number "three" in the three-line break. Some traders prefer to use a two- and others a four-line break. However, three is the most widely used time span. Chart 8-11 shows two-, three-, and four-line break charts in descending order. Note that because time is not a factor in break charts, it is not possible to line them up vertically with identical dates, as you could a bar or candlestick chart. Consequently, they cover slightly different periods. The greater the time span between breaks, the longer the period being covered. The numbers correspond to identical dates and turning points.

If you look closely, you can see that the two-line break chart, which covers the shortest period, offers a substantial number of whipsaw signals dur-

Chart 8-11   D mark and a two-, three-, and four-line break. (Source: *pring.com*)

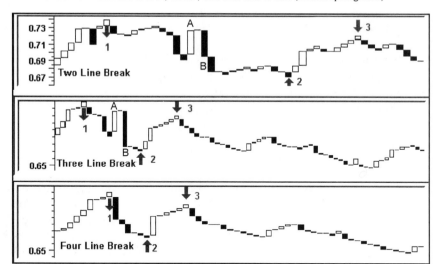

ing the consolidation, which ends with the number 2. There are numerous whipsaws (identified with quick color changes) in the preceding ten blocks.

The three-line break chart in the middle experiences no whipsaws. Finally, with the four-line break chart at the bottom, there are no whipsaws, either.

Finally, consider the period between the numbers 1 and 2. The two-line break chart contains a series of seven waves. The three-line break chart experiences just three waves. Finally, the four-line break chart only experiences one wave, a series of declining black lines. As an indicator of longer-term trends, the four-line chart comes out a head and shoulders above the others. While it is great in terms of avoiding whipsaws, its timing signals leave something to be desired. For example, the sell signal following the peak at the number 1 came at 72c for both the two- and three-line break charts. In the four-line chart, however, it developed at the bottom of the long black line at 69c, fully 3c lower. Having said that, we need to look at the quality of the signals from the three-line break chart. The sell would occur at the bottom of the black day, following the number 1. The next buy develops at the top of the long white day (A), barely breaking even. The next sell would occur with a close below the long white day (B) at the lower end of the very long black day (three blocks before the number 2). Clearly, a substantial loss would be incurred.

The next buy, at number 2, results in a profitable signal for all three charts. However, the actual buy signal for the four-line break chart comes at 70c, whereas the three-line chart triggered a purchase at a relatively better 68c.

As you can see, the results are often determined by the nature of the market being traded. Is it a trading range or trending one? Trending ones favor the four-line break, whereas trading range markets are more suitable for the three-line variety.

Shoes, Suits, and Necks

The three-line break is sometimes used in conjunction with a confirmation. This is where the shoe, suit, and neck come in (Fig. 8-7). In the case of an upside reversal, the last day of the downtrend sometimes appears as a very short black line. This is known as a *black shoe*. In this case, the shortness of the line indicates that downside momentum is dissipating. This is then followed by a long white line, the *white suit*, which tells us that upside momentum is very strong, at least based on the performance of one day. Finally,

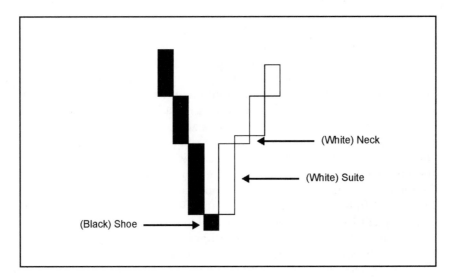

Figure 8-7   Black shoe, white suit, and white neck.

the upside break is confirmed by a short white day, the *neck*, which is literally rising out of the suit. It is the neck that acts as the buy signal, since it confirms the dissipation of downside momentum as reflected in the black shoe. It signals that the long white day, the suit, was not a flash in the pan, but the start of a new trend.

A reversal from an uptrend to a downtrend is signaled in exactly the same way, except that the colors are reversed. In Fig. 8-8 we see a white neck, the last line of the rally. The small vertical size indicates that upside momentum is gradually dissipating, then follows a long black suit, and finally the confirmation with a short black day, the black shoe, follows. This confirms that the sharp decline was not an isolated bear raid, but likely the start of a new trend.

Overbought and Oversold
Three-Line Breaks

There are no formal techniques for determining overbought and oversold lines for three-line breaks. However, many traders mentally, or even physically, count the consecutive number of white or black lines, known as

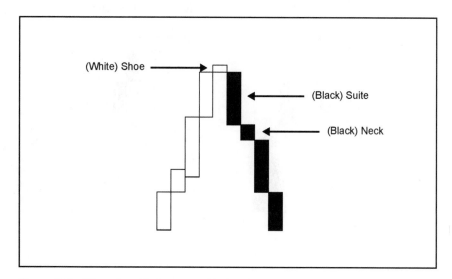

Figure 8-8   White shoe, black suit, and black neck.

"record" days. When the score reaches 8 or 10, the market is considered to be overbought in the case of white lines or oversold in the case of black ones. This approach has especial relevance if, say, after an 8-day advance, the price reaches a resistance level, such as in Fig. 8-9. Alternately, the approach could be expanded to an 8–10-day decline reaching an uptrendline. This could be used as a buying opportunity (Fig. 8-10).

Marketplace Examples

Now it is time to take a look at some market place examples of the three-line break technique in practice. We will also combine this Japanese method with Western charting techniques. In this way, both approaches can be used to gain greater evidence that trend reversals are taking place.

Chart 8-12 features a three-line break example of two very good trendlines for the U.S. Dollar Index. The horizontal line marks the top of a major base. The uptrendline that joins the two lows was violated at point A. Even though prices worked their way higher, the extended line held back all

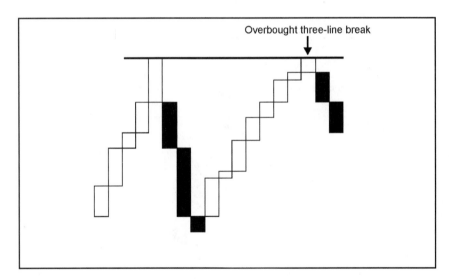

Figure 8-9   Overbought three-line break.

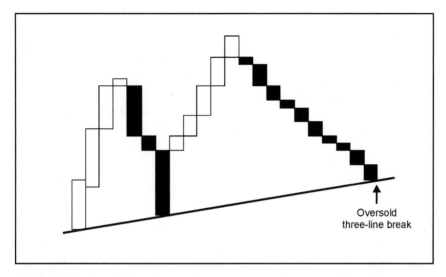

Figure 8-10   Oversold three-line break.

Chart 8-12   U.S. dollar and a three-line break. (Source: *pring.com*)

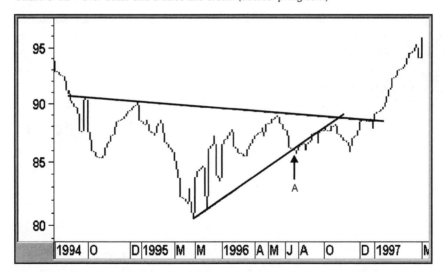

attempts at a rally. It, therefore, marked a very important moving zone of resistance.

A double break offering a very strong buy signal is shown in Chart 8-13. The first break is the downtrendline, which is violated by the very long white line. The second piece of evidence that the trend had reversed occurred when the three-line break moved above the dashed horizontal line. The line is actually the top of a broadening formation with a flat top, a very powerful pattern once completed. The joint simultaneous penetration adds some real strength to the signal, as the Japanese three-line break method is combined with the Western charting technique of trendlines.

Chart 8-14 shows another basing formation. This time it happened to be a consolidation head-and-shoulders pattern, since it was formed during an advance.

Chart 8-15 offers a great example of an oversold three-line break resulting in a rally. Eleven black record days take the price down to support at the trendline. Not surprisingly, a rally develops, but since this is part of an overall bearish trend, the price soon declines again, eventually violating the line. A white neck, white suit, and a black shoe are also indicated in September.

Chart 8-13   March 1996 T. bonds and a three-line break. (Source: *pring.com*)

Chart 8-14   March 1996 S&P Composite and a three-line break. (Source: *pring.com*)

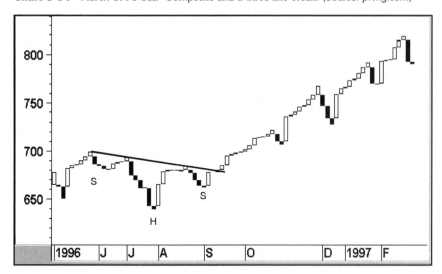

Chart 8-15   Deutsche mark and a three-line break. (Source: *pring.com*)

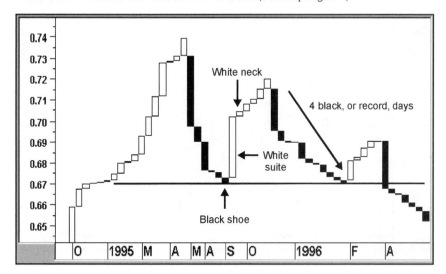

A nice trendline break is shown in Chart 8-16 at point A. An unsuccessful attempt was made to violate the uptrendline at point B. In such instances where a trendline violation is only supported by one day's price action, it is usually best to exit if you use the break as a buying signal. This is because the temporary penetration usually indicates an exhaustion move.

Another trendline violation is illustrated at point C. However, the price quickly moves back above the trendline. Chart 8-17 zeros in on the period of the whipsaw breakdown and shows that this quick reversal was signaled by a black shoe and a strong white suit, followed by a very small neck. This combination not only suggested that the break back above the line was valid, but that a good rally was likely to follow, and one did!

Chart 8-16   French CAC Index and a three-line break. (Source: *pring.com*)

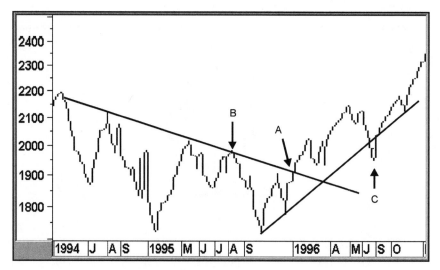

Chart 8-17   French CAC Index and a shoe, suit, and neck formation. (Source: *pring.com*)

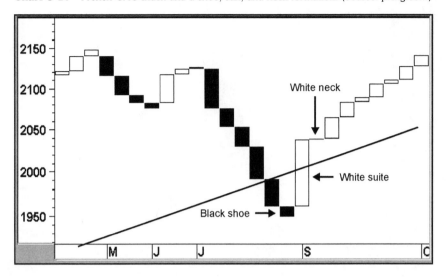

Chart 8-18   Cash cocoa and a shoe, suit, and neck formation. (Source: *pring.com*)

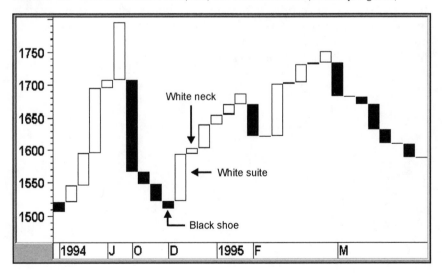

Chart 8-19   Cash corn and a shoe, suit, and neck formation. (Source: *pring.com*)

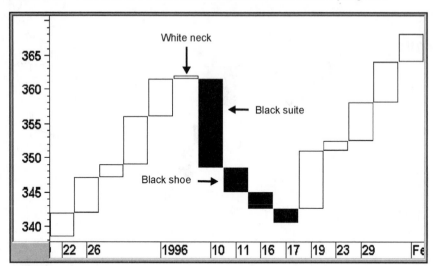

Another example of a shoe, suit, and neck combination is shown in Chart 8-18, this time with cocoa. This formation was followed by a nice uptrend. In Chart 8-19, the corn price experienced a similar pattern; however, this time it is a reversal from an uptrend to a downtrend. In this case, the decline was mercifully short, which is probably as good a place as any to wrap up this chapter on the three-line break.

9

Renko Charts

Basic Construction

Renko charts (Fig. 9-1) are similar in appearance to a three-line break chart. However, there is a major difference in their construction. In a rising three-line break chart, a new white line is added whenever the price makes a new closing-high, by any amount, however small. A renko chart is closer in concept to a point and figure chart, in that a new white line is plotted when the closing price exceeds a previous closing high by a predetermined amount. Just as xs and os in a point and figure chart are all the same size, so each line, or *brick* as they are termed in renko use, is of identical height. Three-line break lines, you will recall, are of differing heights, depending on the degree to which the price rallies or reacts above or below the previous high or low. Thus, with a renko chart, a really strong or weak day could be represented by two, three, or more bricks. For example, if the size of each brick is a dollar and the price closes three dollars above the previous close, that session would be displayed with three white bricks, and vice versa. Remember, renko is only calculated from closing prices, opening; high and low prices are *not* recorded. Consequently, if the price moves up by $4 in intraday and only closes up $2.90, only two bricks would be added, since the price did not attain the $3.00 at the close required for three bricks.

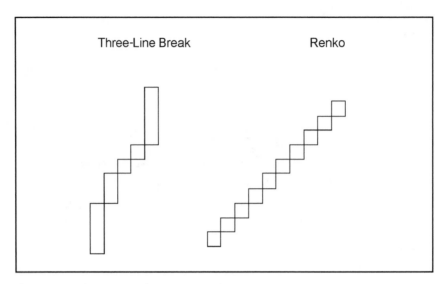

Figure 9-1   Three-line break versus renko charts.

In Fig. 9-2 each brick represents a 2-point price move. The sessions or days are displayed on the left and the price on the right. On Day 2, the price rises from $2.00 to $5.00. Since this is a 2-point renko chart, I can add one brick because the closing price has reached or exceeded the 4-point mark. The plus-one sign indicates the addition of the brick. On Day 3, another rally takes the price to $6.50. You can see that it moves from $5.00 to $6.50, which is a gain of only $1.50, and the height of the brick is 2 points. However, the previous brick reference mark is at $4.00, so $6.50 is more than 2 points above 4, so another brick (Fig. 9-3) is drawn in. Just remember, *it is an increase or decrease from the brick reference point that is important, not the difference between yesterday and today.* Yet another brick can be added on Day 4 because the price now has a closing price of $9.00. The benchmark for another brick is 10, that is, 2 points above the current benchmark of $8.00.

Alternately, a black brick will be added if the price slips below the bottom of the current brick. Right now the top of the current brick is 8, and the brick is worth 2 points, so the bottom is six. Two points below 6 is 4. Thus we have two reference points from which a new brick can be added: a white one, if the price closes at 10 or above, or a black one, if it closes at 4 or below. Nothing happens over the next few sessions because the price remains between 4 and 10. Then, on the tenth session, the price slips to $4.00 and a black brick is added (Fig. 9-4). The decline continues to the 2-point level, and another black brick is added. To add a white brick, the price

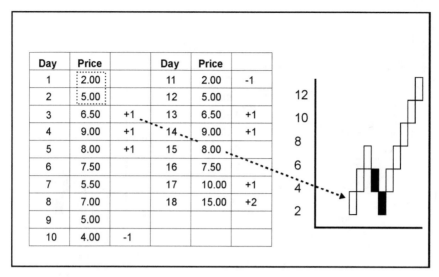

Figure 9-2 Renko calculation.

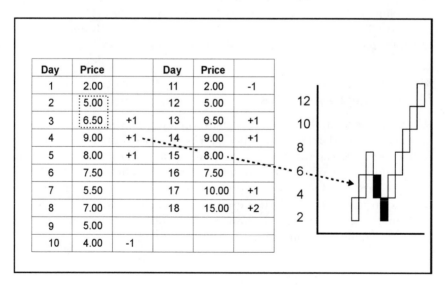

Figure 9-3 Renko calculation.

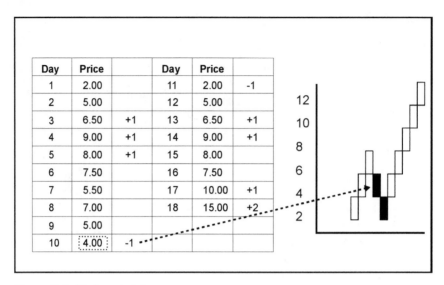

Day	Price		Day	Price	
1	2.00		11	2.00	-1
2	5.00		12	5.00	
3	6.50	+1	13	6.50	+1
4	9.00	+1	14	9.00	+1
5	8.00	+1	15	8.00	
6	7.50		16	7.50	
7	5.50		17	10.00	+1
8	7.00		18	15.00	+2
9	5.00				
10	4.00	-1			

Figure 9-4   Renko calculation.

would need to rally to $6.00 or more. That does not occur until Day 13, when a price of $6.50 is reached. On Day 14, another brick is added because the price moves to the 9-level. Nothing then happens until Day 17, when the price rallies to $10.00. Finally, to end on an optimistic note, the price roars up to $15.00 on the final session, Day 18. Since it is not only above $12.00 but also exceeds $14.00, we can add two bricks on that day.

Marketplace Examples

Renko charts create buy and sell signals when a new white or black brick appears. Chart 9-1 features Coca-Cola. The year 1993 opens with a long series of white bricks, which would have offered a very profitable trade. This would more than offset the countertrend moves indicated by the black bricks. Chart 9-2 of General Motors is also calculated, where each renko brick is worth one dollar. In this example, we see an extremely profitable move in the latter part of 1993. However, if you look closely you will see that there were quite a few offsetting whipsaw moves in 1994.

Chart 9-1 Coca-Cola and a renko chart. (Source: *pring.com*)

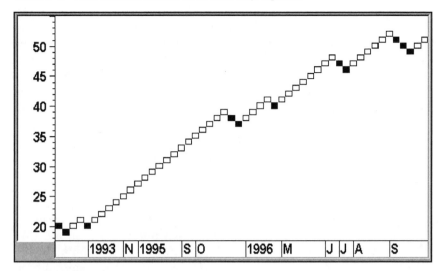

Chart 9-2 General Motors and a renko chart. (Source: *pring.com*)

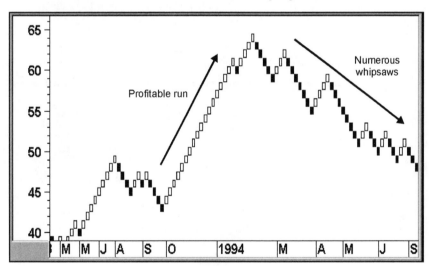

At first glance, you may think that when there are more than three consecutive bricks of the same color, the signal will be profitable. For example,
the left-hand part of Chart 9-3 shows four down days followed by an up day.
The signal to sell short comes at the bottom of the first black brick day. The
buy signal comes at the top of the first white brick. *The difference between the
two lines should be the profit, but there are two caveats.* First, we are assuming that
the closing price is the same at the bottom of the black brick as the top of
the white one, that is, at 62, in this instance. However, since this is a 3-point
renko chart, the close on the black day could have occurred as low as 59.1
and that on the buying white brick .01 point shy of 62. That is a best-case
scenario, which assumes that these bricks represented the closing prices.
However, it is possible to have more than one brick registered on one day.
If the price fell by $6.00 for example, two black bricks would be added.
However, since the bricks are based on closing prices, it is not possible to
know how many bricks will be plotted, until the session has actually closed.
Thus, when you wish to enter a trade, you may find yourself buying after
the second or third white brick following a series of black declining bricks.
In other words, on the type of exceptional day when JP Morgan rallies by
10 or 12 points, use of the closing price to trigger action could easily involve
covering well above the 62-level. Remember, these calculations do not take
commissions and slippage into account. The moral of the story is that profits from these relatively trendy-looking charts are not as good as may appear
from first glance because of the factors just discussed.

Chart 9-3   JP Morgan and a renko chart. (Source: *pring.com*)

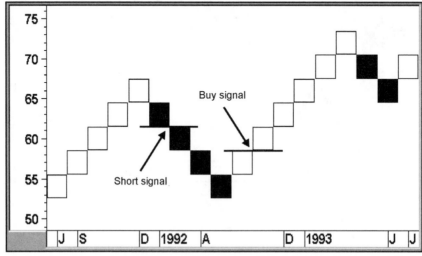

Chart 9-4   JP Morgan and two renko parameters.

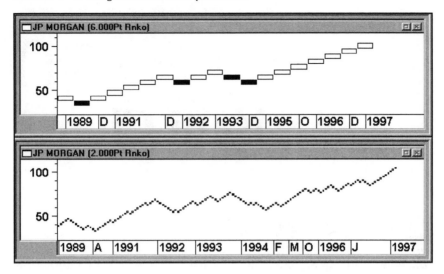

In many respects, the predetermined amounts for the bricks work the same way as the time span on a moving average. The smaller the amount, the more timely the signals: the larger the amount, the less timely but the fewer the number of whipsaws. In Chart 9-4 the bricks have been plotted with a 6-point renko at the top and a 2-point one underneath. You can see how the trends are longer and the whipsaws fewer with the 6-point variety. However, if you remember the caveats concerning the three-color consecutive rule, you can appreciate that the possibilities for slippage are that much greater, too. Although renko charts look pretty seductive, it is well to bear these caveats in mind before entering the market place.

10
Kagi Charts

The Concept

One of the basic tenets of technical analysis is the idea that an uptrend is considered to be in force as long as the price traces out a series of rising peaks and troughs, as in the left-hand part of Fig. 10-1. Similarly, a declining trend is assumed as long as the price traces out a series of declining peaks and troughs. When a series of rising peaks and troughs is broken, a reversal to the downside is signaled, and vice versa. The thinking behind the kagi chart is not dissimilar. The term *kagi* comes from the Japanese word *kagi* that refers to an old-fashioned key with an L-shaped head. As you can see from Fig. 10-2, this is how, in a way, the kagi lines are plotted, as a series of Ls. It is also evident that some of the Ls are thicker than others. *It is the direction of the price trend that determines whether a line is thick or thin.* In this case, thick is up, or bullish, and thin is down, or bearish.

The basis of a kagi chart is the turnaround or reversal amount. The implications are the same as for the renko and three-line break charts, that is, the higher the turnaround value, the fewer the number of whipsaws, but the signals will generally be less timely, and vice versa. When a new high or low for the move is registered, the thickness of the line changes. In keeping with the terminology of oriental philosophy, the thick or rising trend line is called a *yang* and the thin or declining one a *yin*. One final note on terminology: the horizontal lines are known as *inflection* lines.

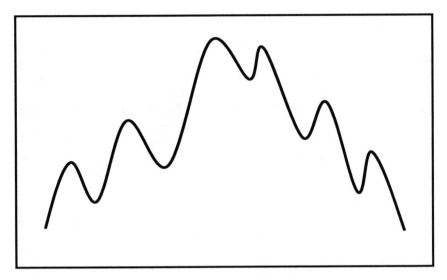

Figure 10-1   Peak-and-trough analysis.

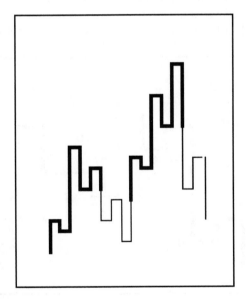

Figure 10-2   How kagis are formed.

Plotting a Kagi

To start a kagi chart, it is first necessary to determine a reversal amount and obtain a closing price that acts as a base price. In Fig. 10-3 this is 1 point. The price starts off at 2 (and rallies to 4.5). However, since the reversal unit is 1 point, the actual kagi line in Fig. 10-3 stops at 4. The price then retreats to 3.5 in the next session, but since this is less than the 1-point reversal amount, it does not show up on the chart. During the next session, the price retreats to 3. Since this is 1 point below the previous benchmark of 4, a downward line is now drawn (point A). This is still displayed as a thick line because the trend is still up. Remember, *the uptrend has to reverse before a thin kagi can appear on the chart.* The next upward kagi takes us from 3 to 8. However, this occurs in two sessions, which are not apparent on the chart. The first day involves a move to 6 and the second to 8. The inflection line at 3 (point A) now becomes an important pivotal point for a decline below 3, because a close below 2 will signal a trend reversal. During the next two days the price rallies to 8.5 and then falls to 7.5. However, neither show up on the chart because both moves are below the 1-point reversal unit. The decline from 8.5 to 7.5 is a full point, but the benchmark is 8 and requires either the price to rally to 9 before the upward line can be extended or decline to 7 before a new downline can start. A decline to 7 develops in the next session (B), followed by a rally to 9. Now the 3-level is no longer the

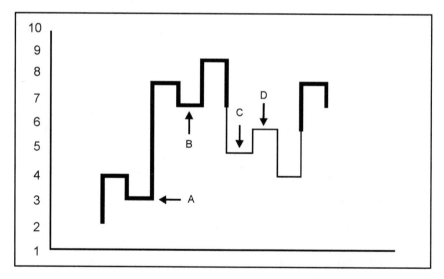

Figure 10-3 Shoulders and waists.

trend-reversal benchmark because a higher low at 7 (point B) has now been established. Then the price hovers between 9.5 and 8.5 for several sessions but none shows up on the chart because the price does not move to 10 or 8, that is, a full point from the benchmark of 9. However, the next day the price falls dramatically to 5. Consequently, the line changes from a bullish thick one to a bearish thin one, as it crosses below the 7, that is, the previous low (arrow at C). A small rally to 6 follows, and then a setback to 4. The 6-level (arrow at D) now becomes important because it represents the previous high. If the price can rally above 6, it will have taken out that high and a thick bullish kagi can then be drawn. That is exactly what happens in the next session, as the price rallies back to 8 again.

Let's quickly recap.

1) Kagi charts use closing prices only.

2) Kagi charts require a turnaround or reversal unit. All plots are made in reversal units. Thick lines indicate a bullish trend and thin ones a bearish one.

3) Once the price has moved by one or more reversal units from the initial starting point, this becomes the benchmark.

4) Only moves equal to or greater than the reversal amount can be used to record a new line or extend an existing one.

5) Benchmark highs and lows are established. When the benchmarks are violated by a different thickness, a new trend is signaled.

Some Examples

Chart 10-1 shows a series of rising, thick inflection lines, that is, the horizontal ones at the left-hand part of the chart. Then the trend reverses, as the kagi moves below the thick inflection line at point A. Once it does then a thin line is plotted. Then we see a rally, but the inflection line remains below the previous thick inflection line, so there is no trend change. The price backs off and the thin inflection line rally peak (point B) now becomes the benchmark. During the subsequent rally you can see that the price thickens up once this benchmark is exceeded. The rally does not last very long, and once C is breached, the trend once again reverts to a negative yin. Point D now becomes the benchmark. As the price slips, so does the benchmark, until it reaches point E, after which a small rally once again results in a reversal.

Chart 10-1   Copper and kagi signals. (Source: *pring.com*)

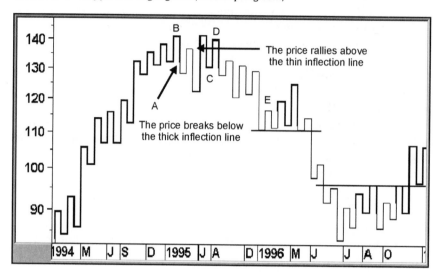

The two trendlines indicate that the kagi inflection lines often throw up good support and resistance points. The upper line, for instance, offers some minor support and the lower one some resistance. It actually forms the top of a price pattern. Note how the retracement move following the breakout finds support at the line.

So far we have discussed reversal amounts as being absolute dollar amounts. However, kagi charts can also be used with percentages. Thus instead of using, say, a 1- or 2-point reversal, it is possible to use a 1- or 2-percent reversal. An example comparing the two methods is shown in Chart 10-2. Historically, this had not been the practice in Japan because percentage calculations are far more tedious to achieve. However, with the advent of computers, it is possible to make either calculation effortlessly. The method is immaterial when applied to small timeframes. However, for charts with longer timeframes, in which a price can double or triple, the percentage calculation is far superior. Just consider, for example, how much more important a $1 move for a stock trading at $5 is, compared to one trading at $20. The first is a 20-percent move, the second 5 percent. In such instances, use of the percentage calculation avoids exaggerating price moves at higher levels.

Chart 10-2   Indonesia fund comparing point and percentage kagis. (Source: *pring.com*)

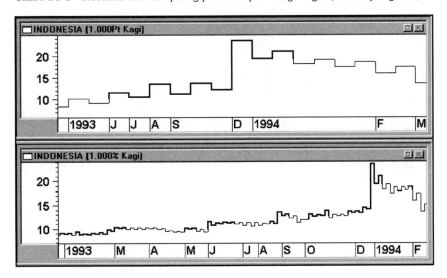

Interpretation

The simplest way to use a kagi chart for market action is to buy when the line goes thick, or changes to a yang, and sell when it changes to a yin. In trading range markets, this approach leads to quite a few whipsaws, because this is a trending tool. That is fairly obvious from Chart 10-3 of the Mexico Fund. Look at the numerous false signals clustered in the area covered by the ellipse on the left, compared to the straight down-run contained within the ellipse on the right.

One technique I have found to be very helpful is to extend the idea of peak-and-trough analysis to the kagi charts themselves. The idea is to study the bullish and bearish periods, as defined by the kagi method. In nearly every established up- and downtrend, the chart alternates between thick bullish lines and thin bearish ones. Remember the idea of a series of rising peaks and troughs in an uptrend and declining ones in a downtrend. In kagi charts, look for a series of rising peaks, as represented by thick inflection lines, and troughs as thin, or yin, lines. The key is to make sure that they both develop at progressively higher levels. In Chart 10-4 the rightward-pointing arrows indicate the thick kagi peaks, which move progressively higher.

Chart 10-3 Mexico fund and line thickness changes. (Source: *pring.com*)

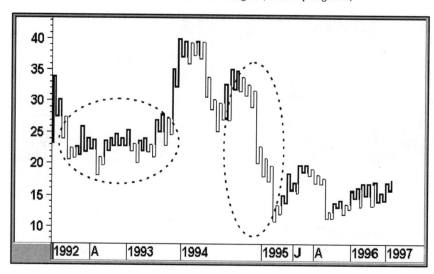

Chart 10-4 Japanese yen and kagi reversal signals. (Source: *pring.com*)

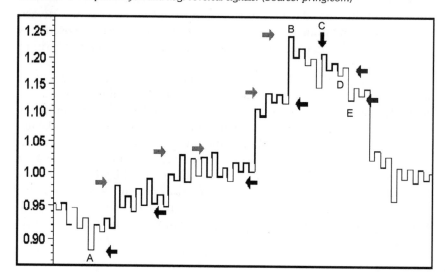

Alternately, the leftward-pointing arrows flag the rising series of troughs, that is, the thin kagi lows. In each instance, starting from point A, the highs are higher and so are the lows. The final peak is reached at point B. After this point, the trend becomes a negative one. But what is the signal? First of all, it is necessary to look for the first thin low, which is indicated at point C. At this juncture, the trend is still officially bullish, since the series of rising lows is still intact. Then a thick rally peaks out at point C. The series of rising peaks is still officially intact, but if this rally fails to take out the final high at point B, that will no longer be the case.

As you can see, the thick line turns to a bearish thin one at point D. Now we know officially that the series of rising peaks is no longer intact, but for an actual reversal confirmation, we need to see the same thing for the troughs. Once the next reaction takes the thin kagi below C, the game is completely up. A new trend has been established where the highs are lower (point C below B) and so are the lows, since point E is below point C.

Chart 10-5 features the Brussels Stock Exchange Index. It begins with a thin kagi low (point A). Then the price takes out its previous high (point B). Next is a thin low (point C), which is higher than the first and then a new thick high (point D). It is at the point just prior to point D, when the line changes from thin to thick, that the buy signal is triggered because we know the series of rising thick highs and thin lows is underway. The thick lines continue unabated until the final peak. The next thin low, at point E, is the first one in a bear trend, but this is not known at the time because the series of rising thick peaks and thin troughs is still intact. The first sign that upside momentum is flagging comes at point F, since it represents a new thin low. Remember, points E and F are separated by a small bullish thick line, so when the line changed from a thick to a thin one just prior to F, the failure of the thick line to make a higher high is confirmed. Up to that point, it was still possible for the thick line to get its act together and make a new high. However, since a new thin line had been established, the series of rising peaks was reversed. Then, when the thin low at F fell below that at E, the trend-reversal signal was triggered.

It is a basic technical principle that once a trend is established, it stays in force, until evidence of a reversal is given. In the next few sessions, we would have been left in some doubt on this question. For example, the next thick line (point G) rallies above the previous one. Since the thick lines were separated by a thin one, this meant that the series of falling peaks had been reversed, almost before they had begun. At point G the series of peaks had been reversed, but not the troughs. Had the next trough at H been above F, then a new uptrend would have been signaled. But that did not occur, and the downtrend resumed.

Chart 10-5   Brussels SE Index and kagi reversal signals. (Source: *pring.com*)

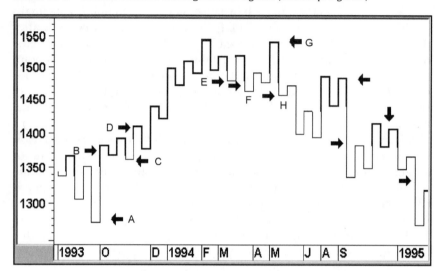

Chart 10-6 shows what happened next. First, at point A?, a rally took the price above the previous thick high. This is the first time that had happened in quite a while. (The question mark is there because at this point, the declining series of peaks has been reversed, but not that of thin troughs.) For a double or complete confirmation, we have to await the next trough, which is at point B, and then a subsequent peak (point C) to confirm that B was, in fact, a valid trough. Since B was above point X, the new uptrend was confirmed as the line thickened just before C. Note that all subsequent thin troughs on this chart now move progressively higher, and all thick kagi peaks achieve the same objective.

Shoulders and Waists

There are two remaining concepts in kagi charting that need to be explained, those of shoulders and waists.

A *shoulder* is an inflection line that was a prior high, and a *waist* is an inflection line of a prior low. One method of interpretation compares these shoulders and waists to preceding shoulders or waists in the prevailing trend. In Fig. 10-4 there is a series of rising shoulders during the uptrend. This indicates a strong market, which is underscored by the fact that the thick waists

Chart 10-6 Brussels SE Index and kagi reversal signals. (Source: *pring.com*)

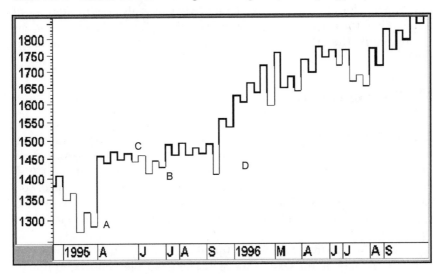

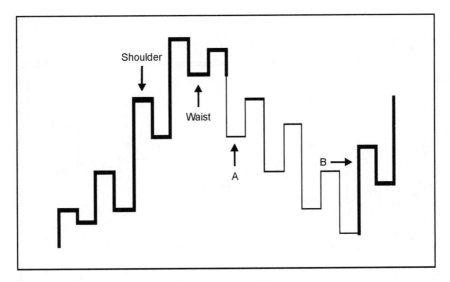

Figure 10-4 Kagi demonstrating shoulders and waists.

are also in a rising trend. Weakness began to appear when the first thin waist developed below the previous thick one (A). This is also the trend-reversal signal. Then the price declines in a series of declining shoulders and waists until point B, when the thick kagi moves above the previous thin shoulder.

Multi-Level Breaks

Since trading range markets can often result in numerous whipsaws, the practice of looking for multiple breaks has arisen. This is really a filtering or confirmation method. For example, in Chart 10-7 of Italian government bond futures, we see a 2-level break to the downside at the first arrow. A *level* is the term that is applied to a previous high or low. In this instance, you can see that the price declined below both points A and B for a 2-level break.

Another two-level break develops in October 1995, but this time it is to the upside.

See how the very long kagi line jumps above the inflection lines at points C and D, and later in the session above E. This was a 3-level break. Although this method decreases the risk of a whipsaw, it also suffers from the draw-back of all filtering techniques, in that valuable profit is given up while wait-ing for the 2- or 3-level break to materialize. One way around this is to only act on these multi-level breaks when the breakout develops fairly close to

Chart 10-7 Italian government bonds and multi-level breaks. (Source: *pring.com*)

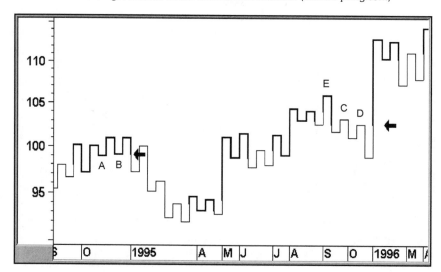

the turning point. In the examples in Chart 10-7, both would qualify, since only a relatively small price increase had taken place at the time of the breakout.

Chart 10-8 shows some more multi-level breaks The long down-kagi at point A broke below three previous lows for a 3-level break. That at point B was a bullish 4-level break. The chart also demonstrates that not all multi-level breaks signal strong trends. The bearish thin kagi at point C, for instance, broke below two prior lows but proved to be a whipsaw. The positive 2-level break at D was also a bad signal as was the negative one at point E.

Corrections Used as Action Points

In Western technical analysis, we often use the 50-percent retracement of a previous rally or reaction as a benchmark (Fig. 10-5). If the price corrects more than 50 percent of the previous advance, it is regarded as a bearish sign, but if a decline holds above the 50-percent mark, this is a positive indication. The reverse would be true for a bear market rally. The arrow with the "100%" next to it indicates 100 percent of the rally from the low to the high. The arrow next to the "50%" indicates the halfway, or 50-percent, mark. The first reaction holds at the 50-percent mark, so the trend is

Chart 10-8 Spain fund and multi-level breaks. (Source: *pring.com*)

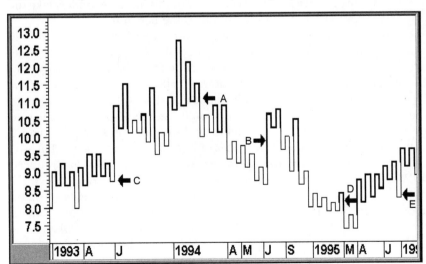

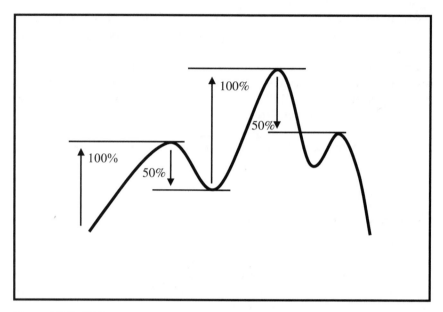

Figure 10-5 50% retracements.

regarded as positive. However, the next decline takes the price below the 50 percent mark, and this is bearish. It is of little wonder, therefore, that when the next rally fails, the price moves to a new low.

Kagi charting also uses a 50-percent rule. In this instance, traders take the 50-percent correction of a long kagi line as the benchmark.

For reference purposes, the halfway points of each kagi chart are indicated with the horizontal tick marks on the right-hand side of the kagi line. The line at A indicates the 50-percent reaction from the previous kagi rally. In this particular instance, the reaction actually goes a little bit below the 50-percent point. That is not really important, since we are trying to get to the spirit of the thing. In effect, we should use the 50-percent rule as an interpretive one based on judgment and commonsense rather than a blindly followed rule. After all, the idea of using 50-percent is somewhat arbitrary. I doubt whether the average trader says to himself, "Okay, it is retraced 50.235, therefore, the trend has reversed." He is more likely to say, "this price has only partially retraced the previous rally, and so far it is held quite a bit above the previous low. As long as it does not fall any further, I will hold on for a while to see what happens." Buyers for their part may say, "Okay, it has retraced quite a bit of the rally and seems to be holding. Rather than wait for a complete retracement, I had better get in now." The idea is not that people are looking for the exact 50-percent retracement but more for a retracement that seems to be under control. That could terminate any-where, say, in the 45–55-percent range. This concept of interpretation and a commonsense application rather than a rigid application of the rules should not be confined to this approach but should be applied to any in technical analysis, be it Japanese candles or any Western technique. Remember, we are trying to judge whether the trend in psychology among buyers and sellers has changed. Rarely does that happen at a specific round number. Returning to Chart 10-9, the actual buying point comes at arrow B, just as the price is breaking above the previous shoulder.

Later on, we see another example, this time from an up- to a downtrend. The first sign of weakness comes when the thick black kagi at D fails to rally above the horizontal line that marks the halfway point of the previous long kagi. Then, as the price declines and the line changes to a thin one at point E, a sell signal is triggered.

Chart 10-10 shows another couple of examples. See how the price decline halts very close to the 50-percent line (arrow A) a couple of times, then rallies above the previous high for a buy signal at the arrow B. Finally, at the top, a rally fails to take the price above the 50-percent mark of a long kagi down day at C. Then, as it falls below the previous waist at arrow D, a sell signal is given.

Chart 10-9 Goldman Sachs commodity index and 50-percent retracements. (Source: *pring.com*)

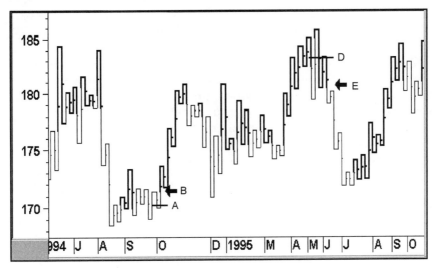

Chart 10-10   Live hogs and 50-percent retracements. (Source: *pring.com*)

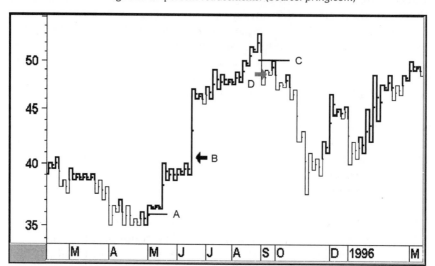

Double Windows

A *double window* is a reversal price pattern. A bullish reversal occurs when a shoulder or series of shoulders forms below a previous waist and the subsequent waist holds above that shoulder. In Chart 10-11 we see a waist (point A) followed by a small rally and reaction. The next shoulder (at point B) forms under the horizontal line, which marks the approximate level of the previous waist. Then a rally develops, but the subsequent waist at C holds above the previous shoulder exactly at the line. It is called a *double window* because the two waists, that is, at points A and C, both hold above the shoulder that separates them.

Chart 10-12 features a variation whereby there are several shoulders that form below the waist at arrow A, just under the horizontal line. In effect, the level at which the shoulders form represents resistance. After the price rallies above the horizontal line, this same level acts as support. Once again we have two waists, at arrows A and B, that hold above a series of shoulders. The shoulders were resistance, but that reverses once the price has rallied above them and they reverse their role to one of support.

Chart 10-11   London Nickel and a bullish double window pattern. (Source: *pring.com*)

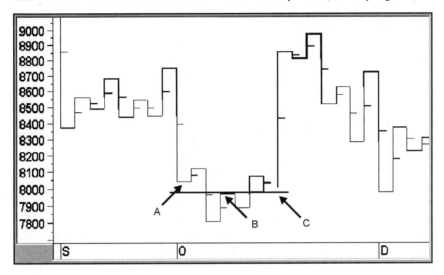

Chart 10-12   London Nickel and a bullish double window pattern. (Source: *pring.com*)

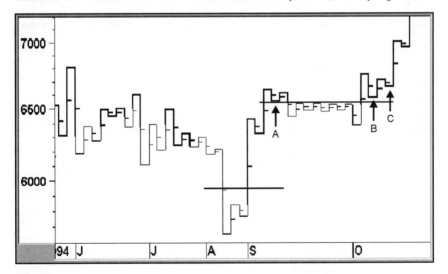

The opposite is true, as an uptrend is reversing to a downtrend where the waists and shoulders reverse their roles (Chart 10-13). The first shoulder in this pattern appears at point A. Then a waist at point B that holds above it. Then a reaction takes place and a shoulder that fails to rally above the waist develops at point C. This double window top was a sign of weakness, so it was not surprising that the price subsequently declined.

Chart 10-14 features the Nikkei Stock Index with another double window top. The shoulder rallies at A and B fail to move above the two thick waists at C and D. This was a particularly interesting pattern because it formed after the price had broken above the March/April line of resistance. Following the breakout it looked as if the price was headed significantly higher. However, the bullish nature of the breakout was completely canceled out by the window top. This just goes to show that it is very important in technical analysis to be as flexible as possible. Once the price had fallen below E it was fairly evident that any long positions placed on the basis of the positive breakout were based on hope, not reality. I would add that it is very difficult to make money out of hope—you really need to have the tape on your side.

Chart 10-13   Nikkei stock index and a double window top. (Source: *pring.com*)

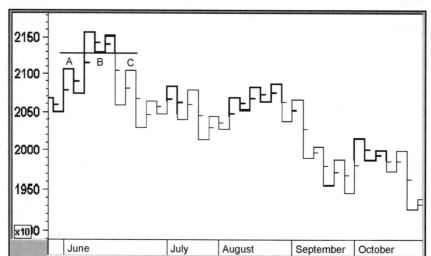

Chart 10-14   Nikkei stock index and a bearish double window top. (Source: *pring.com*)

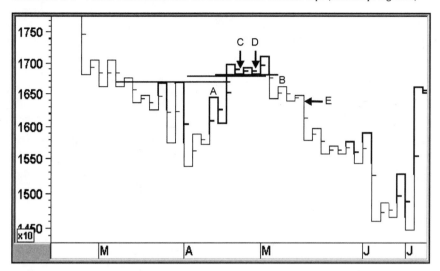

Kagi and Western
Charting Techniques

Kagi charts lend themselves especially well to Western charting techniques, such as price formations and trendlines. This is because kagis are very good at emphasizing support and resistance areas, the basic building blocks of technical analysis. In Chart 10-15 we see a clear-cut top formation at point A. It is arguable what it actually is, since this small rally looks like a right shoulder, so it is not a classic double top. By the same token, the two final rallies end at an identical price level, so it is not a head-and-shoulders top. Whatever it is, the kagi really emphasized the support at this downward-sloping trendline. When it was violated a reversal in trend was confirmed beyond reasonable doubt.

The next formation (point B) is a broadening formation with a flat bottom, a particularly venomous pattern. It was not surprising, therefore, that when the price slipped below the support trendline, all hell broke loose on the downside. The long thin kagi-day of the breakout was also a multi-level break.

Chart 10-15   London 3-month copper and three price patterns. (Source: *pring.com*)

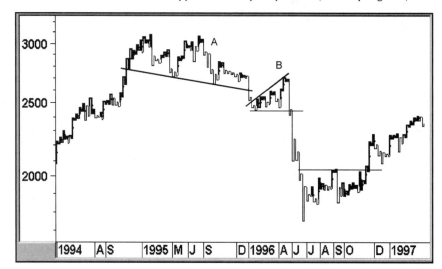

Finally, the kagi displayed a strong resistance level at the horizontal trendline that marked the top of a giant ascending triangle (C).

Using Different Reversal Units

I mentioned earlier that it is possible to construct kagis using different reversal units. Sometimes, it is a good idea to try and experiment with several units of measurements to see what different chart characteristics can be brought out.

The top panel in Chart 10-16 was constructed with a 3-percent point-reversal, and this kagi at the bottom was plotted with a .5-percent reversal unit. Generally speaking, the two top formations look the same, but underneath the surface the differences are quite striking. For example, consider the declining triangle on the .5-percent chart in the October/December period. Now if you look at the same period for the 3-percent reversal chart, you will see a double window top, not a descending triangle. A waist forms above the small horizontal line and the two failed shoulders beneath it. In this instance, both formations are bearish but are distinctly different.

Chart 10-16 London 3-month copper and two kagi variations. (Source: *pring.com*)

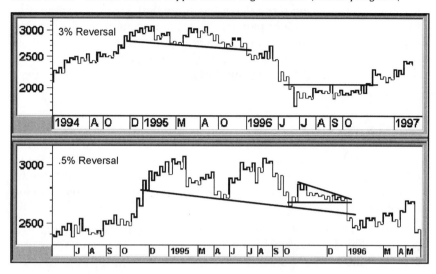

Chart 10-17 Brussels SE Index and two kagi variations. (Source: *pring.com*)

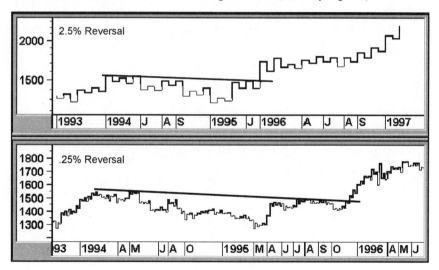

Chart 10-17 of the Belgian stock market features a 2.5-percent reversal at the top and a .25-percent reversal in the bottom. Both scales reflect the large reverse head-and-shoulders pattern. The 2.5-percent scale displays the breakout kagi as a multi-level break, which is good. However, the breakout develops after the move is well underway. Alternately, the smaller-scaled chart still experienced the breakout, but in a much more timely manner.

Kagi Review

1) Kagi charts are constructed as vertical lines whose direction changes when a price reversal from an existing trend of a predetermined amount takes place. These reversal units may be measured in absolute amounts or percentages.

2) Kagi columns or lines are connected by a horizontal line known as a *level*. Levels that develop after a decline are called *waists* and those that develop after a rally are known as *shoulders*.

3) When a kagi penetrates a previous high (shoulder) or low (waist) of a different thickness, the thickness of the line changes. Thin lines are known as *yin*, and indicate downtrends and thick ones as *yang*, and they indicate uptrends. These events can be used as buy and sell signals.

4) Kagis can also signal buy and sell points with multi-level breaks, double windows, and other methods, including some Western charting techniques.

Appendix
Candle Volume Charts

Candle Volume Charts

Candle volume charts are the same as regular candle charts with one important difference. The width of the real bodies varies with the level of volume during that particular session. The greater the volume, the wider the real body, and vice versa. Examples are shown in Fig. A-1. This is a very useful way of presenting the data because the signals from the regular candlesticks are preserved, yet the width of the real bodies offers a quick and simple overview of the volume pattern. Volume is a useful addition to the technical arsenal because it is a totally independent variable from price. For instance, when we look at regular candle charts, renko, kagi, or three-line breaks, these are all different ways of looking at the same thing, namely, price. When we introduce volume into the formula, we are looking at an entirely new aspect. In other words, volume adds a completely new piece of evidence in the weight-of-the-evidence approach discussed at the beginning of this book. One important aspect to consider is the fact that volume reflects an exchange between buyers and sellers. By definition, the amount of money flowing into a security must always equal the amount flowing out. This is true regardless of the level of volume. *It is the level of enthusiasm of buyers or sellers that determines the course of prices.*

Before we take a look at some of these interesting candle variations, it is first necessary to understand a few basic principles of volume interpretation.

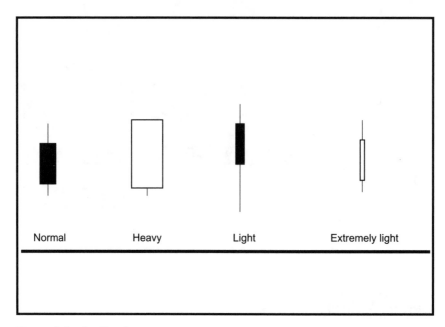

Normal   Heavy   Light   Extremely light

Figure A-1   Candle volume variations.

Interpretive Volume Principles

1. *The most important principle is that volume normally goes with the trend* (Fig. A-2). In a rising market, it is normal for activity to expand, and in a declining one, to contract. In this sense, volume is always interpreted in relation to the recent past. It is no good comparing the current 1-*billion*-plus-shares days on the NYSE with 5 or 6 *million* from seventy years ago. This expansion is a result of institutional changes, a larger market, derivatives, and so forth. However, a two-billion-shares day compared to a recent 1.5-billion-shares day is relevant. Prices move in trends, but do not generally rise and fall in straight lines, as reactions to the prevailing trend set in. The same principle applies to volume. In the left side of Fig. A-2, for instance, the arrow shows that the volume trend is up. By the same token, it is apparent that the level of activity does not expand every day. There are quiet ones and active ones, but the general thrust is upward. The right-hand part of the diagram features a downtrend in volume, but it, too, is irregular. When we talk about volume rising or falling, then we are usually referring to its trend. Volume trends, as with

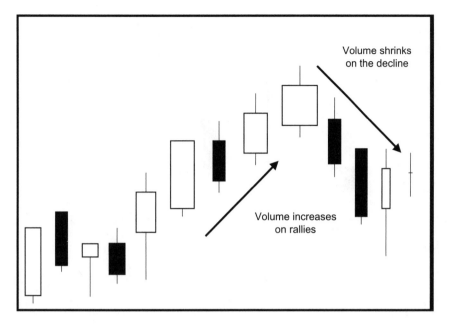

Figure A-2 Normal volume characteristics.

price, can be intraday, short, intermediate, or long, depending on the nature of the chart.

If buyers get greedy, they will push up the bid until they obtain as much quantity as they want. If sellers react to bad news, they might panic, pushing prices down sharply. But at all times the amount of a security being sold is always equal to that being purchased.

Rising volume and price are normal. This combination indicates that the market is "in gear" and has no forecasting value. If this is the case, it is reasonable to expect at least one more rally that reaches a new price high when they are not.

2. *Volume normally leads price during a bull move.* A new high in price that is not confirmed by volume should be regarded as a red flag, warning that the prevailing trend may be about to reverse. In Fig. A-3 the price peaks at point C, yet volume reached its maximum at point A. Such action is normal, the declining volume peaks, warning of underlying technical weakness. As with momentum divergences, there are no hard-and-fast rules about how many divergences precede a peak. Generally speaking,

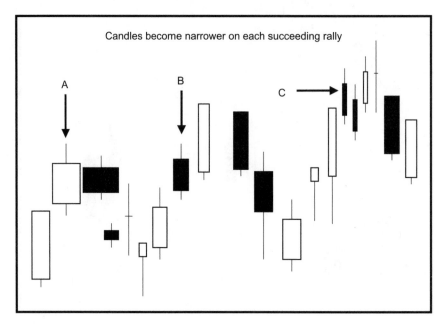

Figure A-3   Volume normally leads price.

though, the greater the number of negative divergences, the weaker the underlying technical picture. Also, the lower the peaks relative to each other, the less enthusiasm being generated and the more susceptible the technical position becomes, once buying dries up or selling-enthusiasm intensifies. A new high accompanied by virtually no volume is just as bearish as a new price-high with virtually no upside momentum.

3. *Rising prices and falling volume* (Fig. A-4) *are abnormal and indicate a weak and suspect rally.* This type of activity is also associated with a primary bear market environment and can be used as an indicator in this respect. Just remember, volume measures the relative enthusiasm of buyers and sellers. A market that rallies on a trend of lower volume indicates that prices are rising because of a lack of sellers rather than the enthusiasm of buyers. Sooner or later, the market will reach a point where sellers become more motivated. After that, prices will start to pick up on the downside. This will show up in candle volume charts as thinner and thinner candles, as the rally gets underway. One tip-off is to watch for volume to increase noticeably as the price starts to decline. That will mean that the candles will get noticeably wider. This is also shown in Fig. A-4.

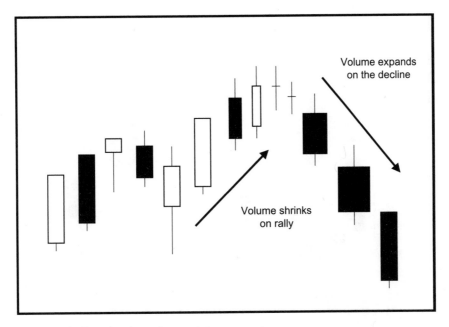

Figure A-4   Bearish volume characteristics.

4. *Sometimes, both price and volume expand slowly, gradually working into an expo-nential rise with a final blow-off stage.* Following this development, both vol-ume and price fall off equally sharply. This represents an exhaustion move and is characteristic of a trend reversal. The significance of the reversal will depend on the extent of the previous advance and the degree of volume expansion. Obviously, an exhaustion move that takes 4–6 days will be nowhere near as significant as one that develops over a matter of weeks. This phenomenon is termed a *parabolic blow-off* and is featured in Fig. A-5. Unfortunately, exhaustion, or blow-off, moves such as these are not easy to define, in the sense that it is possible to construct clearly defin-able trendlines, price patterns, and so on. However, if you are able to spot a couple of extremely long candles with exceptional width on candle vol-ume charts, then this will draw your attention to the probability that the price could be experiencing a parabolic blow-off.

5. *The opposite of a parabolic blow-off is a selling climax* (Fig. A-6). This phe-nomenon occurs when prices fall for a considerable time at an acceler-ating pace, accompanied by expanding volume. Following a selling climax, prices may be expected to rise, and the low established at the time of the climax is unlikely to be violated for a considerable time. A price

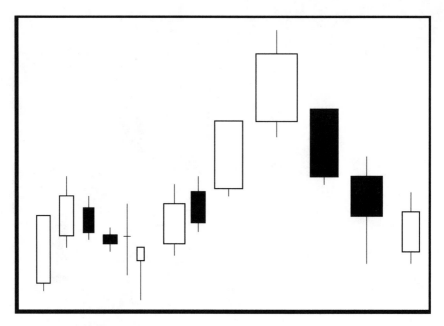

Figure A-5   Parabolic blow-off.

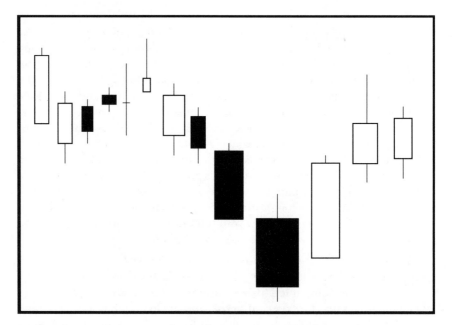

Figure A-6   Selling climax.

rise from a selling climax is by definition accompanied by declining volume. *This is the only time when contracting volume and a rising price may be regarded as normal.* Even so, it is important to make sure that volume expands on subsequent rallies. Termination of a bear market is often, but not always, accompanied by a selling climax.

6. *When prices advance following a long decline and then react to a level at, slightly above, or marginally below the previous trough, it is a bullish sign, if the volume on the second trough is significantly lower than the volume on the first* (Fig. A-7). There is an old saying on Wall Street: "Never short a dull market." It applies very much to this type of situation in which a previous low is being tested with very low volume. This indicates a complete lack of selling pressure.

7. *If an upside breakout develops from a price pattern, trendline violation, and so on, this indicates enthusiasm and is bullish* (Fig. A-8). A downside breakout from a price pattern, trendline, or moving average that occurs on heavy volume is abnormal and is a bearish sign confirming the reversal in trend. When prices decline, it is usually because of a lack of bids, so volume con-

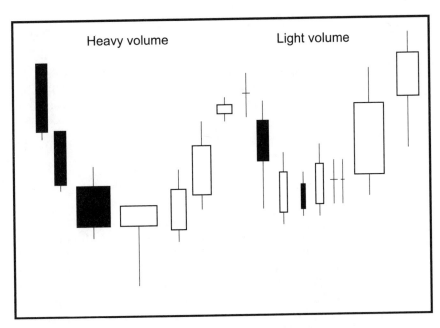

Figure A-7 Low volume on a test.

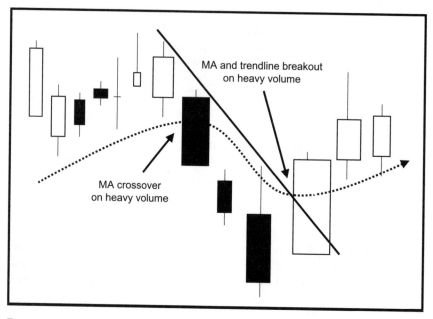

Figure A-8 Volume characteristics on a breakout.

tracts. This is normal activity and is not giving us much information. However, when volume expands on the downside, it is because sellers are more motivated, so the decline, other things being equal, is likely to be more severe.

8. *When the price has been rising for a while, an anemic rise* (Fig. A-9) *accompanied by high volume indicates churning action and is a bearish factor.*

Marketplace Examples

Chart A-1 shows a candle volume chart for Wal-Mart. Notice how the early November window following the bullish engulfing pattern was closed soon after. However, the very thin candles that were involved in the retracement move indicated a lack of volume, which is precisely the type of thing that is required in a pull-back of this nature. Heavy volume in such a situation would indicate selling pressure, as opposed to the situation here wherein prices were clearly falling because of a lack of buying interest.

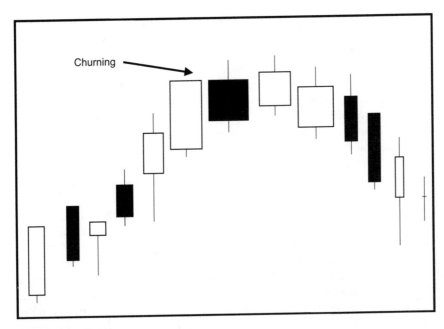

Figure A-9 Churning.

Chart A-1 Wal-Mart and candle volume. (Source: *pring.com*)

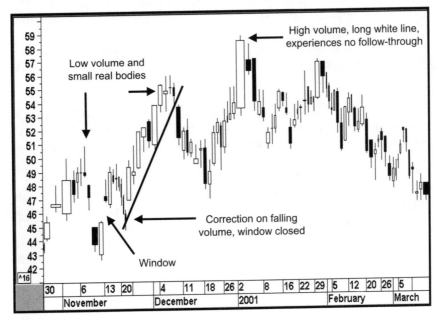

The previous rally experienced a series of very thin candles, which indicated that prices were rising on lower volume. This is opposite to the norm, where rising prices and volume are healthy. The very thin candles, therefore, warned that the days of the rally were numbered.

The late November to early December rally was associated with wider candles, which was a good sign. However, as we reach the week of the 4th the candles move sideways but are very thin. This indicated that the balance between buyers and sellers was more evenly matched. The doji on the day of the high also reflects the even balance. This characteristic is often followed by a trend reversal, especially if volume picks up on the downside. That is precisely what happened here, as the uptrendline is violated and the candles thicken up.

The long, white line that developed at the very end of December looked good at the time, since this candle was a pretty wide one, indicating heavy volume. However, there was no follow-through on the upside, which indicated that the long, white line was a buying climax. This was confirmed first with the establishment of a harami on the subsequent day and by a long black candle that retraced all of the ground gained by the long, white line.

Chart A-2 features a candle volume chart of Microsoft. Note that from the 30th of November the bulk of the candles are thin, indicating low volume. The only thick candles are black ones, which signifies potential selling pressure. Finally, the right-shoulder rally consists of thin candles, indicating low (bearish) volume. The early December bear rally is also associated with thin candles. Rising prices on weak volume is bearish because it indicates that prices are rallying on a lack of selling rather than enthusiastic buying. Then, on the day of the rally high, the relatively thick black candle indicates the days of the bulls are numbered because selling pressure has started to pick up.

You can see that the February downtrendline break (Chart A-3) is associated with a thick belt-hold and a trendline break in the RSI. Also, it is important to note that the nature of the RSI changes with candle volume, because the wider candles involve a slower, more deliberate price action by the oscillator. Thin lines work in the opposite way, of course.

Chart A-4, featuring Boeing, shows an engulfing day in January. It is a thick candle, and the high volume that this reflects adds to the bearishness of the pattern. Finally, note how the candles break out from a symmetrical triangle at the same time that the RSI completes a base.

Chart A-2 Microsoft with candle volume and an RSI. (Source: *pring.com*)

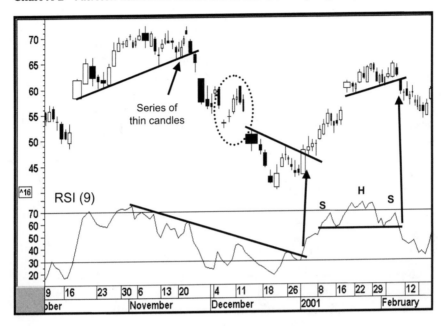

Chart A-3 Microsoft with candle volume and an RSI. (Source: *pring.com*)

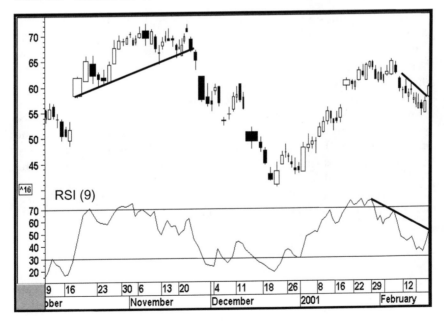

Chart A-4   Boeing with candle volume and an RSI. (Source: *pring.com*)

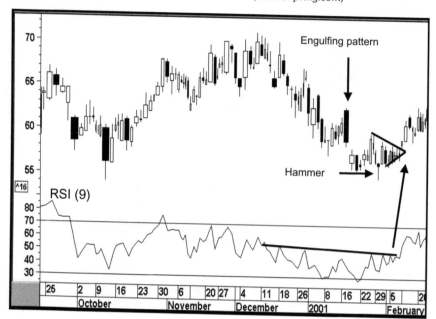

Chart A-5 features a downside breakout in Allegheny Tech in July 2001. Note how most of the candles at the May/June top were extremely wide, indicating lots of volume. However, the price made almost no headway, thereby indicating a classic example of churning. This was confirmed as the price broke below the trendline and the 25-day MA

American Express, in Chart A-6, experienced a classic triangle bottom in summer 2001. The narrowing trading range indicated that the balance between buyers and sellers was becoming very evenly matched. However, the narrowing nature of the candle volume reinforced this fact by indicating that volume was really shrinking. Thus, there was a total lack of interest in the stock. Then, when the price broke out, the white candle was noticeably wider than its predecessors, indicating a significant pick up in activity, as the balance tipped strongly in favor of the buyers.

Chart A-5 Allegheny Tech and candle volume. (Source: *pring.com*)

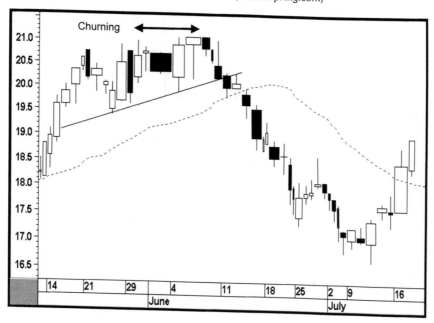

Chart A-6 American Express and candle volume. (Source: *pring.com*)

Chart A-7   American International Group and candle volume. (Source: *pring.com*)

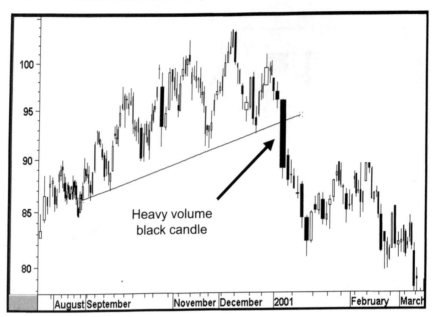

American International Group, in Chart A-7, breaks down from a top in early 2001. The nature of the break is significant because the long, black candle was also much wider than anything seen previously on the chart. Long black candles on downside breaks are usually significant, but the heavy volume was the icing on the bearish cake.

Candlestick Charting Quiz

1. Japanese candlestick charts:
   - A.) Are generally used for short-term trading.
   - B.) Have been used in Japan for several centuries.
   - C.) Are not perfect, but represent a useful adjunct to the technical arsenal.
   - D.) All of the above.

2. The real body in a candlestick is represented by:
   - A.) The high and the low.
   - B.) The opening and the closing price.
   - C.) The high and the close.
   - D.) None of the above.

3. Candlestick charts place the greatest emphasis on the:
   - A.) High and the close.
   - B.) Low and the opening.
   - C.) High and the low.
   - D.) Opening and the close.

4. Which of these candles in the following figure is a hanging man?
   - A.)
   - B.)
   - C.)
   - D.)

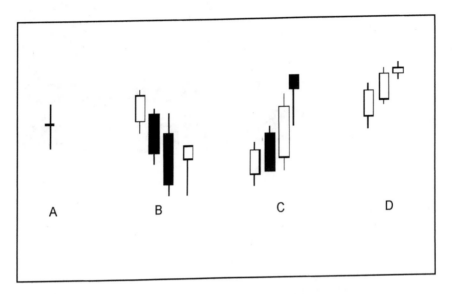

5. Which of these formations is a bearish shooting star?
   A.)
   B.)
   C.)
   D.)

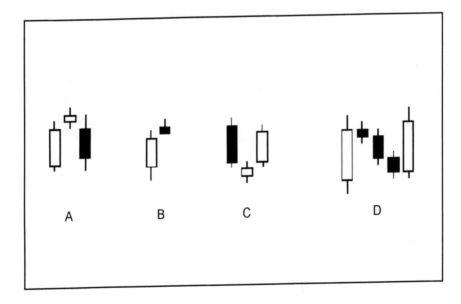

6. Which of these patterns is a piercing white line?
   A.)
   B.)
   C.)
   D.)

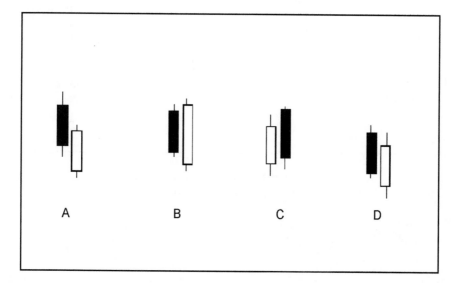

7. Which of the following is the pattern with the correct identification?
   A.)
   B.)
   C.)
   D.)

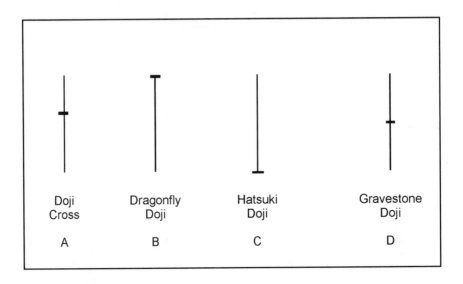

8. Which of these patterns is the upside-gap two crows?
    A.)
    B.)
    C.)
    D.)

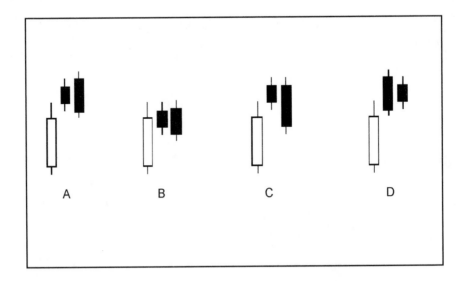

9. Which of these is the tower bottom?
    A.)
    B.)
    C.)
    D.)

10. Which of these patterns is a fry pan bottom?
    A.)
    B.)
    C.)

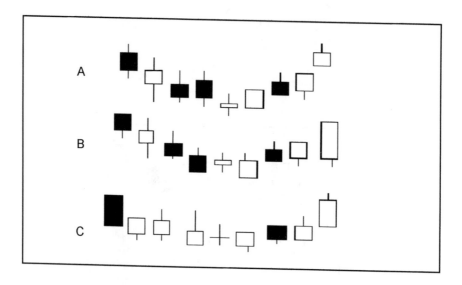

11. This pattern is:
   A.) An inverted Buddha.
   B.) A three-rivers bottom.
   C.) A dumpling bottom.

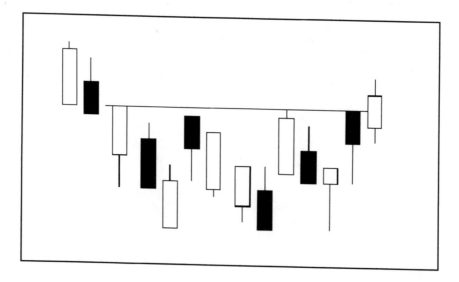

12. Which of these patterns is a three-mountains top?
   A.)
   B.)
   C.)

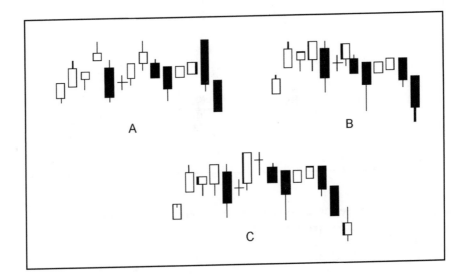

13. Which of these patterns is the bullish counterattack line?
   A.)
   B.)
   C.)
   D.)

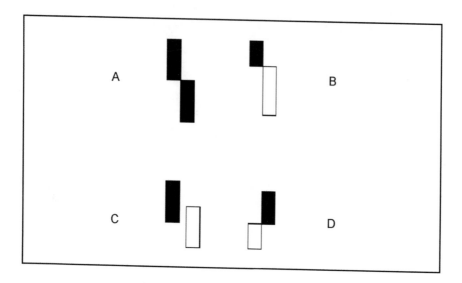

14. Which of these formations meets the strictest requirements of the
three black crows pattern?
A.)
B.)
C.)
D.)

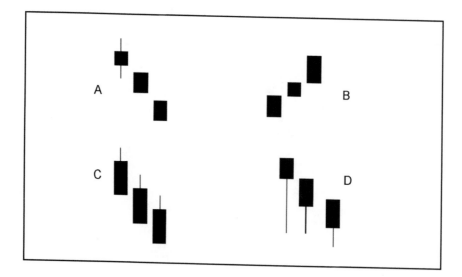

15. What is this pattern?

    A.) A matt-hold.

    B.) An engulfing pattern.

    C.) A piercing line.

    D.) A harami.

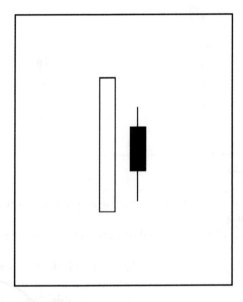

16. Which of these patterns is a harami?

    A.)

    B.)

    C.)

    D.)

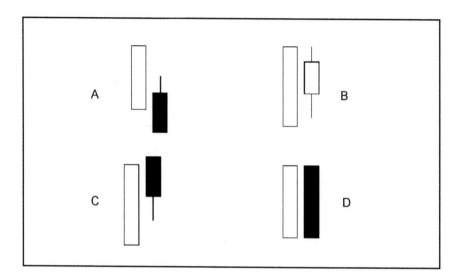

17. Which of these descriptions best applies to a tweezer top?
  A.) It is a long-term top.
  B.) It consists of two side-by-side candles where the real bodies are the same height.
  C.) It consists of two or more days in which the highs are more or less identical.
  D.) A top on which the second day totally engulfs the first.

18. Can an engulfing pattern ever be the same as a tweezer bottom?
  A.) Yes
  B.) No

19. What kind of pattern is this?
  A.) A rising three methods.
  B.) An upside-gap tasuki.
  C.) A high-price gapping play.
  D.) A regular gap, or window.

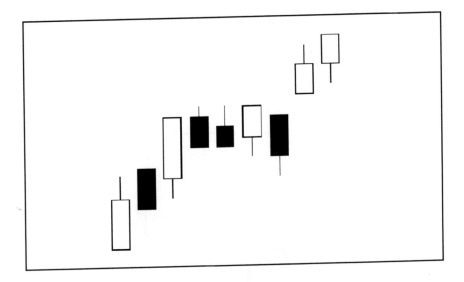

20. Which pattern is the correct falling three methods?

A.)

B.)

C.)

D.)

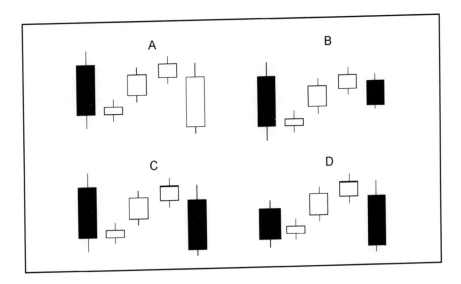

21. What pattern is shown in this chart?
   A.) A stalled three white soldiers.
   B.) Two white soldiers and a gap.
   C.) Gapping side-by-side white lines.
   D.) An upside tasuki gap.

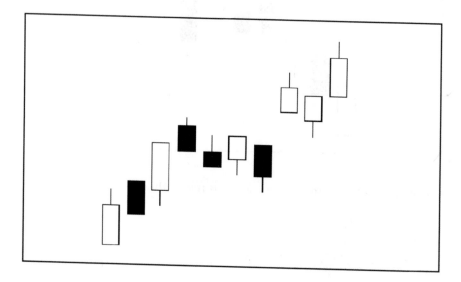

22. Which of these formations is an advancing three white soldiers pattern?
   A.)
   B.)
   C.)

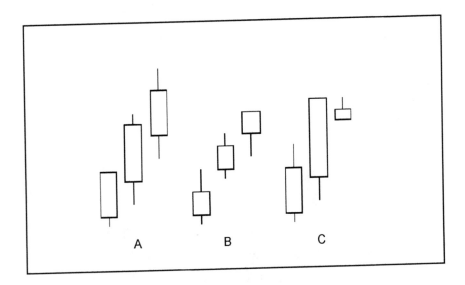

23. True or false: Since reversal patterns signal trend reversals, they never appear in the charts as continuation patterns.
   A.) True
   B.) False

24. A separating line:
   A.) Consists of two candles of differing colors that close at the same level.
   B.) Consists of two candles of the same color that close at the same level during an uptrend.
   C.) Consists of two candles of differing colors that open at the same level.
   D.) Consists of two black candles that open and close at different levels.

25. Which rally contains a separating line?
   A.)
   B.)
   C.)

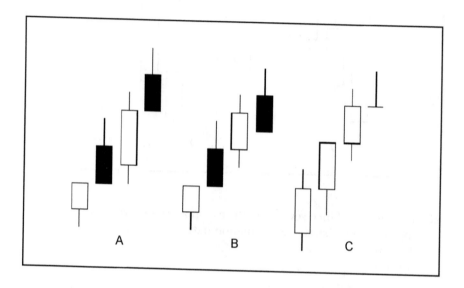

26. Which group of candles represents a rising three methods formation?
   A.)
   B.)
   C.)

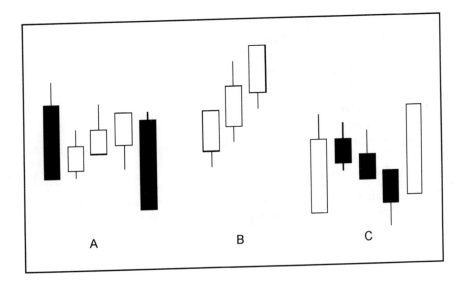

27. Which candle group contains a gapping side-by-side white lines?
    A.)
    B.)
    C.)

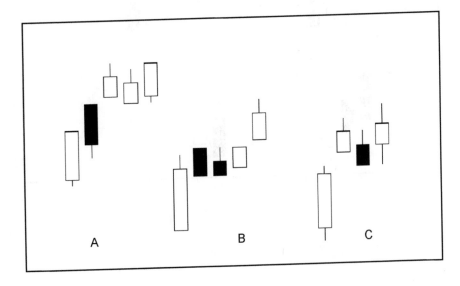

28. Which is more bullish?
  A.) A bullish engulfing pattern.
  B.) A negative trendline break.
  C.) A bullish piercing line and a positive trendline break.
  D.) A hammer.

29. Which, in a relative sense, is the most reliable pattern?
  A.) A three-buddha top.
  B.) A Western head-and-shoulders top.
  C.) A and B.
  D.) Two consecutive haramis.

30. Assuming each of the trendlines is of equal significance, which pattern is likely to offer the strongest resistance?
  A.)
  B.)
  C.)
  D.)

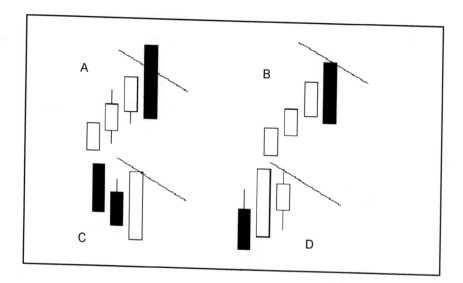

31. An overbought reading in a short-term momentum indicator combined with a hanging man indicates:

   A.) A sharp sell-off is extremely likely.
   B.) The next day will be a gravestone doji.
   C.) The market may be vulnerable, and we should keep an eye out for more signs of trouble.
   D.) The price will go up because the bullish hanging man will more than offset the bearish potential of the overbought reading.

32. The thick lines are identical moving averages. Which of these situations is likely to be followed by a positive crossover?

   A.)
   B.)
   C.)
   D.)

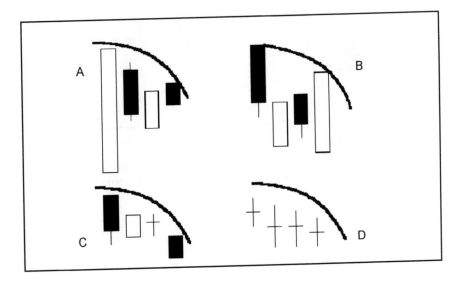

33. One of the characteristics of a white belt-hold is:

   A.) It tends to be very bullish after a decline.
   B.) The opening price will often become a key support area on a subsequent decline.
   C.) Trend breaks and moving average crossovers are more likely to be sustained than on an ordinary candle day.
   D.) All of the above.

34. The price declines to an uptrendline. Which of the following is more likely to be followed by a negative violation in the next session?
A.)
B.)
C.)
D.)

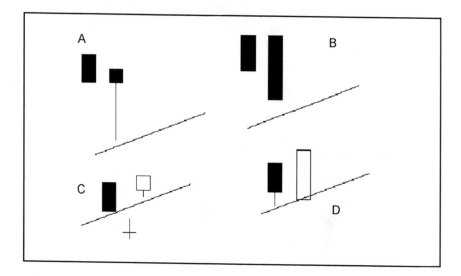

35. Which of these examples is most likely to result in a decline? For your information, the indicator at the bottom is a short-term oscillator.
A.)
B.)

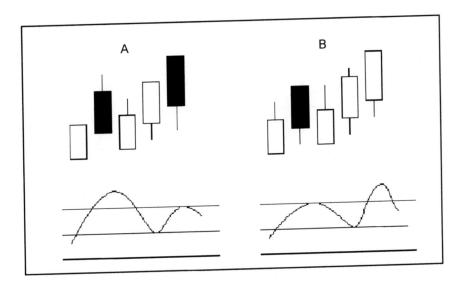

36. When are opening prices important in three-line break charts?
  A.) When the close is above the opening.
  B.) When the opening is above the close.
  C.) A and B.
  D.) None of the above.

37. In this bullish three-line break chart below, at which point should the price close for a black turnaround line to be drawn?
  A.) Below line A.
  B.) Below line B.

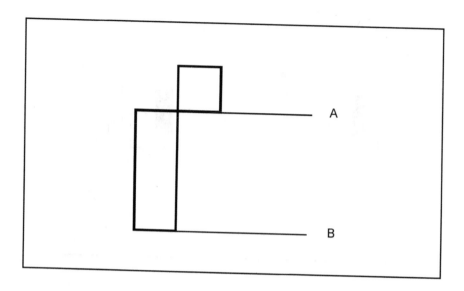

38. In this three-line break chart, where would the next white turnaround line be plotted?
- A.) Above line D.
- B.) Above line A.
- C.) Above line B.
- D.) Above line C.

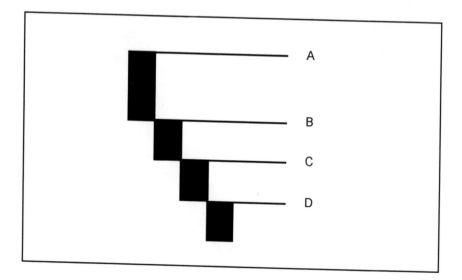

39. In this three-line break chart, the price reverses and makes a closing
high at $10. Which event would trigger a new white line?
- A.) Two consecutive intraday highs at 20.
- B.) A new intraday high at 20.
- C.) A close at 11.
- D.) A close at 9.

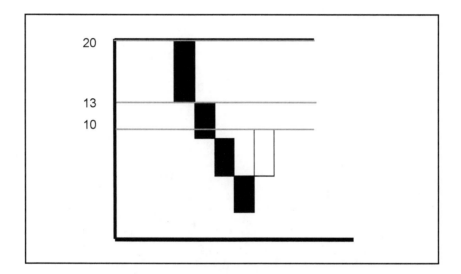

40. A three-line break chart reverses to the upside. We buy at $10 and
decide to liquidate when a new series of black lines develops. The
actual reversal signal would be a close below $9. Ignoring
commissions and assuming there is no price slippage in the execution
of our order at the closing price, which of these statements is true?
- A.) Our loss will be limited to $1, that is, $10 minus $9.
- B.) Our loss will be less than $1.
- C.) Our loss will be greater than $1.
- D.) Our loss could be $1 or it could be more.

41. Why is the three-line break chart generally more useful than a two- or
four-line break?
- A.) Because it has been in use in Japan for over 300 years and other
break charts have only been in use in the last couple of decades.
- B.) Because the number 3 is very important in Japanese charting.
- C.) Because it represents a good trade-off between timeliness and
sensitivity.

42. Three-line break charts should be used:
    A.) On their own.
    B.) In conjunction with any other indicators, where appropriate.
    C.) Only with Western charting techniques.
    D.) Only with Japanese candles.

43. Which chart offers the stronger signal?
    A.)
    B.)

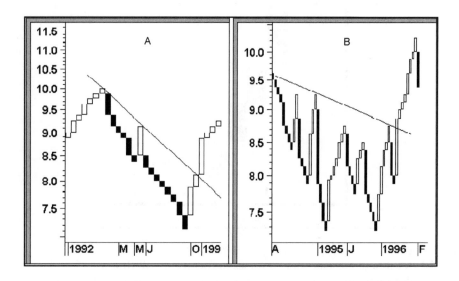

44. Which example has just violated support?

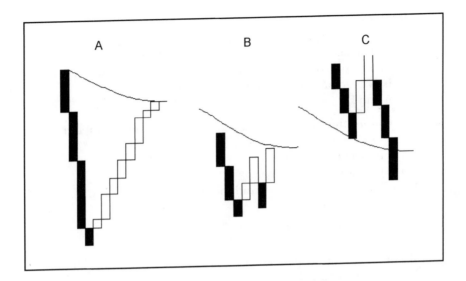

45. Which of these statements is correct?
   A.) Time and opening prices are not important in three-line break charts.
   B.) Time and closing prices are both critical in three-line break charts.
   C.) Patience and discipline are important in the interpretation of three-line break charts.
   D.) A and C.

46. What is the principal difference between a renko and a three-line break chart?
   A.) Renko bricks are of equal height and are added whenever a price makes a new closing high or low for the move. Three-line break lines are of differing height depending on the size of a move.
   B.) Renko bricks are added every time a new intraday high or low is achieved. Three-line break charts are only based on closing prices.
   C.) Renko charts use point-and-figure techniques, three-line break charts do not.
   D.) None of the above.

47. A Renko brick:
A.) Can, under special circumstances, be of differing height in the same chart.
B.) Can be one of several bricks that are added in one session.
C.) Is occasionally part of an engulfing pattern.
D.) A and B.

48. What is the advantage of setting a large predetermined amount for a renko brick?
A.) The signals are timelier.
B.) There are fewer whipsaws.
C.) The signals are timelier and there are fewer whipsaws.
D.) None of the above.

49. Kagi charts are constructed from:
A.) The high, low, and close.
B.) The high, low, open, and close.
C.) The open and close.
D.) Closing prices only.

50. In this chart, above which line would the kagi line change from thick to thin?
A.)
B.)
C.)
D.)

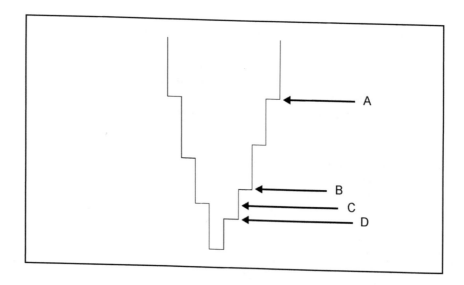

51. What pattern, if any, is completed when this kagi breaks above the point marked by the arrow?
   A.) A two-level break.
   B.) A three-level break.
   C.) A double window top.
   D.) A double window bottom.

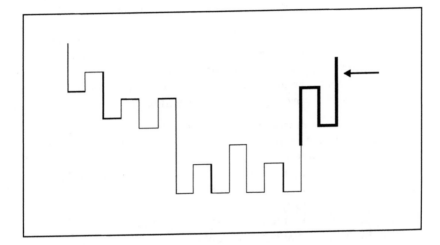

52. What pattern, if any, is completed when this kagi reverses to a thick bullish line?
   A.) A two-level break.
   B.) A three-level break.
   C.) A double window top.
   D.) A double window bottom.

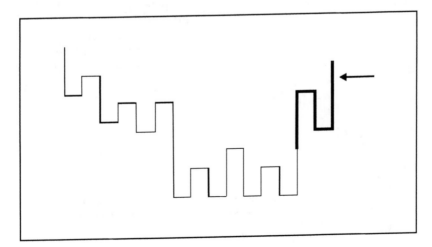

53. A shoulder in a kagi chart is:

   A.) An inflection line that was a prior low.

   B.) An inflection level that was a three-line break.

   C.) An inflection line during a decline.

   D.) An inflection line that was a prior high.

54. Which of these statements is true?

   A.) A price that retraces more than 50% of an advance is always in a bear trend.

   B.) A price that reverses more than 50% of an advance indicates that the trend may have reversed but should be interpreted with some flexibility and a degree of commonsense.

   C.) Fifty percent is an absolutely critical point, since a retracement of 50.001% of a move signals that the trend has reversed.

55. With the benefit of hindsight, we know that the early 1994 high was the top. However, at point X on the chart, was the trend in a strict technical sense defined as:

   A.) Negative, because the series of declining thin waists was down.

   B.) Negative, because the series of declining thin waists and shoulders was down.

   C.) Negative, because the price had already retraced more than 50% of the advance that began in July 1993.

   D.) Positive, because the series of rising thick peaks had not yet reversed and a trend reversal requires that both must reverse before a trend reversal signal is given.

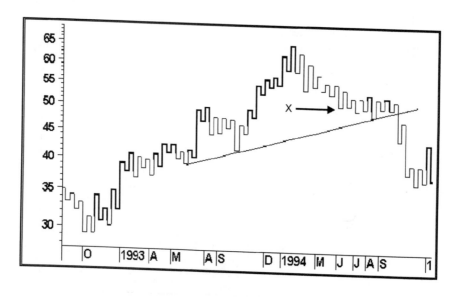

Candlestick Charting Quiz

56. There are several factors that make this chart bearish at point X.
Which statement best describes them?
   A.) The price retraced more than 50% of the rally that began in July
       1993.
   B.) A series of declining peaks and troughs has been established and
       the price has broken down from an upward-sloping head and
       shoulders, that is, a three-buddha top.
   C.) The price has completed a three mountains top.
   D.) The price has completed an upward-sloping head-and-shoulders
       top and retraced more than 50% of the rally that began in July
       1993.

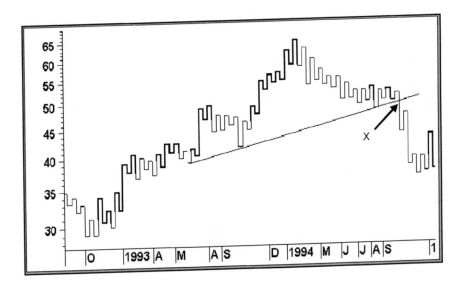

Candlestick Charting Quiz Answers

(For a full description of the answers, please refer to the Quiz section on the CD-ROM contained at the back of this book.)

1. D
2. B
3. D
4. C
5. B
6. D
7. B
8. A
9. C
10. A
11. B
12. A
13. B
14. C
15. D
16. B

17. C

18. A

19. C

20. C

21. C

22. A

23. B

24. C

25. B

26. C

27. A

28. C

29. C

30. A

31. C

32. B

33. D

34. B

35. A

36. D

37. B

38. C

39. C

40. D

41. C

42. B

43. B

44. D

45. D

46. D

47. B

48. B

49. D

50. C

51. D

52. B

53. D

54. B

55. D

56. B

Index

About the Author

Martin J. Pring is the highly respected president of Pring Research (**www.pring.com**), editor of the newsletter *The Intermarket Review,* and one of today's most influential thought leaders in the world of technical analysis. Pring has written more than a dozen trading books and has contributed to *Barron's* and other national publications. He was awarded the Jack Frost Memorial Award from the Canadian Technical Analysts Society.

THE INTERMARKET REVIEW

is a 34+ page monthly publication which will keep you current on the U.S. Bond, stock, and precious metal markets. Each issue also contains up-to-date information on currencies, international debt, equity markets and commodity indices.

This is the only source that uses Martin's 6-Stage Business Cycle approach. The business cycle has seasons just like a calendar year. Each of the six distinct stages, or seasons, can be used to create new investment opportunities and reap their profits. The InterMarket Review identifies these stages and explains how they will affect your portfolio. Martin provides specific asset allocation recommendations, along with market developments you need to be aware of.

EVERY MONTH YOU WILL RECEIVE IN-DEPTH COVERAGE OF:

- Martin's personal Barometers for the Bond, Stock and Commodity markets. These unique indicators have identified all major turning points in the postwar period, usually on a very timely basis and have outperformed the buy/hold approach by a wide margin.

S&P Composite and the Stock Barometer

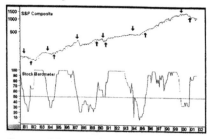

Barometers help organize the economic data that recognize

- Chart Watch - features the market Martin feels is poised for a major move.

- Pring Turner Stock Report - insights from Joe Turner of Pring Turner Capital Group, on a stock they are monitoring for their portfolio considerations.

- Martin's Personal Portfolio Recommendations - Every issue has at least 6 stocks Martin feels are a potential purchase. Long- and short-term charts are here, along with buy recommendations!

Backed by over 30 years of Martin's personal technical experience providing analysis for key brokerage firms, developing indicators, investing in markets and learning from the past, you're sure to find the InterMarket Review educational and informative.

*Please visit **www.pring.com** to sign up for a 3-month trial and view an issue!*

Installation Instructions

This CD has an Autorun feature. Insert the CD into the CD-ROM drive and it will start automatically. Please allow sufficient time for loading.

If the Autorun feature does not work, insert the CD, open your CD-ROM drive and double-click on the Setup.exe icon. Then, access the program by clicking on Start, Programs, Pring and locate the icon for the tutorial title you are playing in the flyout.

1. We recommend not changing the default installation settings.
2. This program is best viewed using small fonts.
3. This CD is best viewed in 800 × 600 pixels and 256 colors.
4. For additional support, please go to Support at **www.pring.com**.

Advanced Technical Analysis CD Tutorials:
Learning the KST

Intro to Candlestick Charting

Tech's Guide to Day Trading

Breaking the Black Box

How to Select Stocks

MetaStock CD Tutorials:
Exploring MS Basic

Exploring MS Advanced

Super CD Companion

Indicator Companion

Market Analysis Companion

Selecting Stocks Using MetaStock

*Visit **http://www.pring.com** for info on these and other products.*

Pring Research, Inc.
1539 S. Orange Avenue, Sarasota, FL 34239

800-221-7514 • 941-364-5850

Internet: www.pring.com • E-mail: info@pring.com